Help Us to a Better Land:
Crofter Colonies in the Prairie West

Help Us to a Better Land:
Crofter Colonies in the Prairie West

Wayne Norton

Canadian Plains Research Center
University of Regina
1994

Canadian Plains Research Center
University of Regina
Regina, Saskatchewan S4S 0A2
Canada

Canadian Cataloguing in Publication Data
Norton, Wayne R. (Wayne Reid), 1948-
    Help us to a better land
    (Canadian plains studies, ISSN 0317-6290 ; 25)
    Includes index.
    ISBN 0-88977-078-6
1. Scots - Prairie Provinces - History - 19th century.
2. Prairie Provinces - Emigration and immigration -
History - 19th century. 3. Highlands (Scotland) -
Emigration and immigration - History - 19th century.
I. University of Regina. Canadian Plains
Research Center. II. Title. III. Series.

FC3250.S3N67 1994   971.2'020049163   C93-098214-2
F1060.97.S4N67 1994
Cover Design: Brian Mlazgar/Agnes Bray

Printed and bound in Canada by
Hignell Printing Limited, Winnipeg, Manitoba
Printed on acid-free paper

Dedication

To the memory of the uncertain settlers from the Western Isles and their reluctant administrators this book is dedicated.

"[To] put the matter bluntly, it is better and cheaper for the state to assist a certain number of people to make a living in a new land than to have either to support them at home or allow them to starve."

Glasgow Herald, 21 April 1888

"[The crofter scheme] is not in any way aided or particularly invited by the Department. It is purely an Imperial tentative effort."

John Lowe, Deputy Minister of Agriculture, 1890

"We should never have come."

John McKay to Sir Charles Tupper, 1893

Contents

Dramatis Personae

GEORGE BETTS BORRADAILE. The son of a Canadian customs agent, G.B. Borradaile was born in Halifax in 1861. He joined the North West Mounted Police in 1876 (smudging his age on the application) and remained with the Force until 1879. He was married in Winnipeg in 1885 after having served as a Steele Scout in the North-West Rebellion, and worked as a surveyor until 1889. Having returned to Halifax, Borradaile received the appointment to meet the 1889 crofters in April. His original instructions were to accompany them to the West and to assist in their settlement. In July, he was appointed as Crofter Commissioner, a position he retained until 1905. After a series of serious illnesses, Borradaile and his young family moved from Winnipeg to Medicine Hat in 1900. There he became a justice of the peace and died in 1908.

JOSEPH GROSE COLMER. Born in 1856 in London, J.G. Colmer emigrated to Canada and was appointed to the Canadian civil service in 1880. He was Sir Alexander Galt's private secretary from 1880 to 1882 and became Permanent Secretary to the Office of the Canadian High Commission in 1883. He was appointed Secretary to the Imperial Colonisation Board in 1889, a position he did not formally relinquish until 1926. Colmer served under three High Commissioners: Sir Alexander Galt, Sir Charles Tupper and Sir Donald Smith (Lord Strathcona). He resigned as Secretary to the Office of the High Commission in 1903 to take a position with a firm of London stockbrokers. He was a member of Joseph Chamberlain's Tariff Commission in 1904 and Honorary Secretary of the Canada Club for twenty-six years. His obituary in *The Times* (London) credited Colmer with having moved "Englishmen away from the idea that Canada was only furs and lumber and quarrels." He died in 1937.

THE CROFTERS. The seventy-nine families who settled with British government assistance near Pelican Lake and Saltcoats, were generally referred to as "crofters." Strictly speaking, however, the majority of the adult males had been fishermen and cottars (cottagers without tenurial rights) rather than crofters (tenants of small land holdings) in the Western Isles. Their decision to emigrate changed their lives dramatically, and their settlement difficulties destroyed the very government policies the crofters had been selected to promote.

LORD LOTHIAN. Schomberg Henry Kerr was born in 1833, and became the ninth Marquess of Lothian in 1870. The title brought with it dominion over 32,000 acres in southeastern Scotland. Lothian had an undistinguished career at Oxford and in the diplomatic service, but became

Secretary for Scotland in Lord Salisbury's second administration in March 1887. He was committed to maintaining the privileges associated with property in late Victorian Scotland, and his sponsorship of the emigration scheme of 1888 was motivated by this commitment. Lothian's term as Secretary for Scotland ended with the return to power of Gladstone's Liberals in August 1892. He died in London in 1900.

SIR MALCOLM MCNEILL. Born on the island of Barra in 1839, Malcolm McNeill was educated at Eton and Sandhurst. Noted for his military bearing, he nevertheless retired from army life in 1861. After temporarily emigrating to New Zealand, McNeill entered the civil service in 1867, taking a position with the Board of Supervision for the Relief of the Poor and of Public Health in Scotland. A life-long advocate of emigration as a solution to Highland problems, he initiated the emigration scheme adopted by the Scottish Office in 1888. McNeill, a Gaelic speaker, was secretary to the Napier Commission in 1883. He became Secretary of the Board of Supervision in 1892, Secretary of the Local Government Board in 1894, and Vice-President and Chairman of the Local Government Board in 1897. McNeill was knighted in 1901, retired in 1905, and died in Edinburgh in 1919.

SIR GEORGE TREVELYAN. Born in 1838, Trevelyan's extensive career included achievements in literature, historical writing, and politics. First elected to the British Parliament in 1865 as a reform-minded Liberal, Trevelyan received his first cabinet appointment in 1884. He served briefly as Secretary for Scotland in 1886, and was responsible for introducing Gladstone's crofter legislation. He returned to office in 1892, succeeding Lothian as Secretary for Scotland. His disapproval of government-assisted emigration led him to cancel the crofter colonization scheme in 1893. He remained as Scottish secretary until 1895, and retired from politics in 1897.

SIR CHARLES TUPPER. One of the original fathers of Confederation, Charles Tupper was born in 1821 at Amherst, Nova Scotia. He held a series of portfolios in the governments of Sir John A. Macdonald. He "retired" to take the position of Canadian High Commissioner in London in 1884. Tupper remained in this position until 1896, but was in Canada during the critical period in 1887-88 when the crofter colonization scheme was being formulated. Deeply concerned with Canada's reputation in Britain as a field for emigration, Tupper sought to present the crofter settlements in the most favourable light possible. He was a key member of the Imperial Colonisation Board from 1889 until 1896, when he returned to Ottawa to become Canada's sixth prime minister. Tupper died in England in 1915.

Foreword

The story of the Scots in North America, which spans three centuries, begins with the early European voyages of discovery. In the British North American colonies after 1800 people of Scottish origins made up 10 to 15 percent of the total population. In certain of the colonies the percentage was much higher; in Nova Scotia for example, those with a Scottish background comprised 33.7 percent of the population in 1871. Continued immigration from Scotland assured that the Scots would remain one of the major ethnic components of the Canadian population. Moreover, this immigrant group possessed a remarkably resilient sense of identity that had grown from a long tradition of selective resistance to the assimilative pressures of an Anglo-Saxon majority. Their self-conscious ethnicity, along with the immediately significant role played by immigrant Scots in Canadian business, political, religious and educational life assured their prominence in the nation's historical memory. Indeed, the size of the Scottish-Canadian cast of characters presented in the standard Canadian history text stands as testimony of the extent to which the Scots in Canada have been the subject of historical analysis and discussion.

Though there is a considerable literature relating to the Scots in Canada, it must be noted that Norton's study is more than just another traverse over old ground. His examination of crofter settlers and the Imperial Colonisation Board complements the existing Scottish-Canadian historical canon in that it addresses one of the dominant traditional themes — immigration and settlement, and especially that old and much laboured topic — Scots in the West. European penetration and settlement of the Canadian West began with Scots, especially those in the employ of the North West Company. The exploits of Alexander Mackenzie and Simon Fraser are common knowledge, as is the story of Lord Selkirk's Red River colonists. Acknowledged as the first European settlers in the Canadian prairie West, Selkirk's colonists are the subject of *The Red River Settlement* (1856), the first history of western Canada, written by the immigrant Scottish fur trader, settler and historian, Alexander Ross. From his worthy predecessor Norton picks up the tale of sponsored immigrant Scottish settlers on the Prairies almost three generations later. It is this late nineteenth century time frame that makes Norton's study unique and of particular significance. It is not just that the traditional literature says so little about Scottish settlement in Canada after 1870, but also that the experience of the crofter settlers sent to

Pelican Lake and Saltcoats, along with that of their British sponsor, the Imperial Colonisation Board, had an important influence upon the thinking of the Canadian and British governments about immigration policies at a critical moment in the history of both countries.

On a more human and more personal level, the story of the Pelican Lake and Saltcoats crofters at the close of the nineteenth century, like that of the Red River colonists at the beginning of the century, is a moving account of a people's efforts to adapt in order to survive in a new and strange land. Unlike the tradition begun by Ross and others that endowed the Scots above all immigrant groups with those qualities necessary for success on the North American frontier, Norton suggests that the attitudes and practices brought by the crofters from the Western Isles in fact may have inhibited the necessary process of adaptation. Whatever may be said of these early prairie homesteaders, one thing is clear, their story has a contemporary resonance. On prairie farms many of their descendants still cling precariously close to the margin as they continue the search begun by their forebearers for the necessary adjustments to ensure survival in a harsh land.

Norton's study of the crofters at Pelican Lake and Saltcoats informs more than just an audience interested in prairie settlement and the Scots in Canada, important as these topics are. The crofters' experience is also part of a much larger story. Norton's book has a legitimate place in the historiography of Scotland and of the Scots overseas. It also fits comfortably within the body of literature devoted to British colonial policy. In this context, the author offers the important observation that the apparently less than successful attempt to establish crofter settlements on the Canadian prairie may have dissuaded Imperial policy makers from further ventures of this kind, even at a time when there was no lack of enthusiasm for other more costly Imperial ventures. This suggestion will certainly interest Imperial historians.

Wayne Norton is to be complimented on a finely crafted and engaging commentary that will no doubt attract both popular and academic readers. He has presented an important work deserving of a wide audience.

David H. Breen
University of British Columbia

Preface

EMIGRATION looms as large in the history of Scotland as does immigration in the history of Canada. For both countries, the migration of population has resulted in changes in their respective societies and economies. Traditionally, those interested in the fate of Scottish emigrants to Canada have focussed upon either eastern Canada or the business class, or both. The generally accepted stereotype of the Scots in Canada is one of a favoured people who stepped from the decks of the *Hector* into the board rooms of the nation's industries after only brief apprenticeships.

But most Scottish immigrants shared the struggles, successes, and disappointments that awaited other newcomers to this country. This was as true of the earlier Scottish settlers in Nova Scotia and Upper Canada as it was of the later emigrants to the coalfields and wheatfields of the West. In the late nineteenth century, the British government initiated a rather curious scheme of settlement on the Canadian Prairies, specifically for Highland Scots. The settlement scheme is truly the forgotten episode in the history of the Scots in Canada. The emigration portion of the scheme, too, has been almost entirely neglected by Scottish historians. It is hoped that this study will be a step toward ending this neglect on both sides of the Atlantic.

The settlements established in 1888 near Killarney and in 1889 near Saltcoats had a profound influence on public policy in both Scotland and Canada. The idea of assisted emigration from the Highlands in the 1880s was a highly charged political issue, and the selected emigrants were pawns in the game of "emigration roulette" played by Scottish authorities. Canada's governments were never able to determine just what their role was to be in this "purely Imperial tentative effort." The settlers themselves quickly found that their common purpose was simply to survive in a strange land, and that there would be nothing simple about the attempt.

This book could not have been written without the assistance and encouragement of many people. I am grateful to my advisors at the University of British Columbia: David Breen, James Winter, and Fritz Lehmann. I am indebted to a large number of correspondents, most notably Stuart Macdonald, Marilyn Lewry, Marjory Harper, and Ian Levitt. Several relatives and descendants of those whose story is told here have provided me with valuable information and photographs. I must particularly mention Lois Klaassen, Jim Jowsey, and Osmond

Borradaile in this respect. Indispensable advice was received from librarians, archivists and keepers at the Scottish Record Office (in particular David J. Brown of the West Search Room), the National Archives of Canada, the Saskatchewan Archives Board, the Provincial Archives of Manitoba, the Vancouver City Archives, the University of British Columbia, the J.A.V. David Museum at Killarney, the Medicine Hat Museum, the Saltcoats Museum and Manitoba Land Titles offices. Financial assistance from the J.S. Ewart Fund at the University of Manitoba, from the Atlantic Canada Study Group, and from the University of British Columbia made research trips possible. The research assistance of Linda Wolfe, Ronald Watson and Krina Forbes was much appreciated, as was the photographic assistance provided by Majory Harper, Donald Paterson and Norman Little in Scotland and by Wilf Schmidt in Canada. On many occasions, Andrew Yarmie and Doreen Stewart provided both necessary assistance and cheerful counsel. The diligent attention to detail by the staff at the Canadian Plains Research Center has improved the manuscript in numerous respects. For this, I gratefully acknowledge the work of Agnes Bray, Donna Achtzener and Brian Mlazgar. Any and all errors contained herein are, of course, entirely my own responsibility.

Finally, to my wife Val, thank you. This would not have been possible without you.

Wayne Norton
Kamloops, British Columbia

Introduction

THE GREY SKIES over the Western Isles of Scotland were familiar. But for the passengers aboard the *Claymore*, the prospect of never seeing those skies again was entirely new. They had surprised their friends, their government, and probably themselves by accepting the offer of a loan to assist their emigration to an unspecified location on the Canadian Prairies. The day of departure, 14 May 1888, had arrived. On the quay, a middle-aged man of military bearing was deep in discussion with an angry shopkeeper, delaying the *Claymore*'s departure on its regular run from Stornoway to Glasgow.

The anxious emigrants, waving to friends and relatives on the quayside, used the delay to reflect on the events and circumstances that had led them to the remarkable decision to abandon beloved crofts for a destination unknown. That decision had not been made lightly, but it had been made hastily. Just eight days earlier, they had heard their church ministers announce from the pulpits throughout the island of Lewis that a representative of the British government was in Stornoway to receive applications for assisted emigration to Canada. In exchange for a promise to repay a loan of £120, each family head was to receive title to a grant of 160 acres of farmland in Canada! The size of the grant was breathtaking when compared to the poor, pitiful crofts upon which they toiled for so little return. In addition, wages in the fishing industry, the island's chief source of income, recently had collapsed. The prospects for the poor on the island of Lewis, never bright, had become bleak in the 1880s.

Earlier in the year, when delegations of crofters had met to discuss grievances with Lady Matheson, the owner of most of Lewis, they had been told that how she ran her estates was no concern of theirs. Lady Matheson then left the island for Paris, but not before two detachments of marines had arrived in Lewis to suppress a series of disturbances caused by hunger and destitution. The gunboat HMS *Jackal*, occupying the adjacent berth in Stornoway harbour, was a grim reminder that the island was still under military occupation.

The discussion on the quay ended. The shopkeeper pocketed some money, and the other man prepared to mount the gangplank. Before doing so, he hailed several people clinging to their baggage on the quayside. As he offered each a last chance to board the *Claymore*, each solemnly declined. This was Malcolm McNeill, known to all present as a Poor Law official from Edinburgh. On special leave from his regular duties, he had heard dozens of applications for emigration assistance during the previous week. He had made his selections, and now he was angered that several of these were refusing to embark at the last moment.

Instructions were given, and the *Claymore* was finally able to cast off. On board were several of the major players in the crofters' drama. Malcolm McNeill, the originator of the settlement scheme now under way, firmly believed that a general emigration from the Western Isles would resolve the problems of poverty and overpopulation that plagued the islands in the late nineteenth century. Thomas Grahame, the Glasgow agent of the Canadian government, hoped that the venture would draw to the Canadian Prairies the increased emigration that had failed to materialize after the completion of the Canadian Pacific Railway in 1885. As the *Claymore* reached open water, the two men, deep in optimistic conversation, could not have known how quick and how bitter their disappointments were to be.

The other ninety-five passengers, the first in nearly four decades to leave the Western Isles with government assistance, cast their hopes forward to Canada and their eyes firmly back to Stornoway until the town, and then the island, faded from sight. There had been no time to arrange for the sale of goods and chattels. Most of the emigrants possessed little more than a change of clothes and the debt of £120 to the British government. John McLeod of Lasdale grieved that, at the last moment, his youngest daughter refused to accompany the rest of the family. Murdo Stewart of Coll regretted that his sister had made the same decision. John Nicolson of North Shabost had arranged a quick marriage and was able to persuade McNeill to add his new wife, Jessie, to the lists of emigrants. The Nicolsons were to have nine children in Manitoba. We can only hope that they ultimately regarded the Canadian West as the better land they were seeking, for the present writer has been unable to determine if they ever saw Lewis again.

Three separate dreams were therefore in conjunction that May morning. For Scottish government officials, the dream was of the voluntary depopulation of the troubled Western Isles. For the Canadians, the vision was that a populated, productive West would bring stability and prosperity to the young nation of Canada. For the emigrants, the dream was the same as that held by the millions who had crossed the Atlantic before them: a better life in a better land. A brief look at the connected histories of both Scotland and Canada is necessary to see how this conjunction of dreams and dreamers had come about.

It had been nearly three centuries since Scots first attempted to establish colonies in British North America. Though the tentative settlements in Nova Scotia in 1622 did not create an immediate flow of emigrants, the eventual settlement in Atlantic Canada of both Highland and Lowland Scots is well known and well documented. As the nineteenth century progressed, dozens of other Canadian locations saw the establishment of Scottish colonies, of which Glengarry and Red River are the most famous. If the overwhelming majority of new arrivals were poor, other social classes were well represented in the emigration, and the reputation of Scots as desirable immigrants was soon established by their preponderance in the entrepreneurial, political, and professional realms.

The experience of all immigrants is profoundly affected by the local circumstances of their new communities. So, too, do the factors determining the decision to emigrate vary from region to region, from estate to estate, from island to island, and from year to year. Still, some generalizations are possible. In Scotland, two distinct traditions are divided politically, economically, and socially by the Highland Line. In the Highlands and Islands, the process of agricultural modernization met with a much more tenacious people and social structure than it encountered in the east and south of the country. The history of emigration from the Highlands and Islands contains a legacy of bitterness and betrayal that contrasts sharply with the process of emigration from the rest of the country. But the policies and practices of the landed interests that resulted in what are generally referred to as "the Highland clearances" also varied dramatically both temporally and geographically.

Lewis and Harris certainly did not escape the evictions and clearances that swept across the Highlands in the late eighteenth and early nineteenth centuries. But like the whole of the Western Isles, they were more affected by the turmoil caused by the failure of successive potato crops in the 1830s and 1840s. The landlords saw migration as the only means to rid their estates of tenant populations who had become, more than ever, a drain on their resources. On Harris, soldiers assisted in the removal of the cottar population in 1839; on Lewis (also known as the Lews), after the passage of the *Emigration Advances Act* in 1851, the James Matheson estate forced hundreds of families to accept assisted passages to Australia under the terms offered by the Highland and Island Emigration Society. This organization had been created to reduce Highland poverty by reducing the population through a policy of emigration. The chairman of the society was Charles Trevelyan, then with the Treasury, and his assistant was John McNeill, a Scottish Poor Law official. Ironically, it was to be McNeill's nephew who would initiate the emigration scheme of 1888; even more ironically, Trevelyan's son would cancel it.

After a quarter of a century of relative security, the problems of poverty and overpopulation again presented themselves in the 1880s, especially on the islands, and this time accompanied by a vociferous and organized demand for the return of land and rights to the tenant populations. It was against this background that Lady Gordon Cathcart decided to assist the emigration and colonization of a small number of families from her Benbecula estates. Amendments to the Canadian *Dominion Lands Act* in 1881 and 1883 permitted a sponsor to lend the sum of $500 to each emigrant committed to settling on the Canadian Prairies. The advance was to cover passage, subsistence, and farm costs. The example set by Lady Cathcart's colonies at Wapella and Moosomin drew much attention from all those interested in addressing Britain's population problems and particularly from those concerned with the renewed Highland discontent in the late 1880s.

The Canadians, of course, did not see the alleviation of Highland discontent as part of their political agenda. What was wanted was a populated prairie region to complement the other planks of the National Policy. The government experimented with a wide range of measures to encourage prairie settlement after Sir John A. Macdonald returned to power in 1878. Assisted passages, promotional literature, sponsored lectures, tenant-farmer tours, railway land grants, colonization companies — all were adopted (and modified with alarming frequency), but were only marginally successful during the 1880s. The provisions of the *Dominion Lands Act* attracted a number of sponsors. However, all the resulting colonies remained very small and none was expected to lead to a substantial migration to the Canadian Prairies. The proposals emanating from the Scottish Office after 1886 held out the possibility of a much greater promise.

CHAPTER ONE

Origins

IN CONFIDENTIAL reports submitted in 1886 to the newly created Scottish Office, a Poor Law official described the social, economic, and political conditions in the troubled Highlands and Islands of Scotland. Acknowledging that the tenant population was solidly opposed to leaving its home parishes, the official nevertheless included in one report an outline of a scheme of state-aided emigration:

> It may not be out of place here to describe the mode in which I should propose to conduct a State-aided scheme...
>
> The leading features of the scheme should be made known by advertisement, proclamation from the pulpit, and printed notice throughout the Highlands; I should then take no further steps to entice applicants, but should proceed to select suitable families from Benbecula, South Uist, and the Lewis. These families I should embark, in the principal port of their district, in a specially-fitted steamship, which would be thrown open to inspection, and to which I would convey the emigrants and their baggage, from outlying townships, in a tender. After providing for all the suitable families anxious to remove, I should take no further steps to popularize emigration, except by circulating printed information, and by visiting the townships to confer with those who preferred personal interviews. I should rely on the effects of letters from the first emigrants, and, if this were as I anticipate, the selection of suitable families would remain the only duty of any importance.[1]

The reports had been requested by an administration uncomfortable with the approach taken by its Liberal predecessor in dealing with continued distress and disorder in the Western Isles. The recommendation regarding emigration, and the Poor Law official who made it, would not go unnoticed.

HIGHLAND DISCONTENT AND THE NAPIER COMMISSION

The causes contributing to Highland discontent in the 1880s were essentially the same as those that had resulted in the extensive migrations and emigrations of the previous century. The new political order after 1745 had stripped certain classes of their social significance. The tacksmen, for example, had fulfilled a military and middle management role. Usually related to the laird, they organized the clan for his military purposes, and rented his land to sublet to the tenant population. As the substance of these roles disappeared, the tacksmen were the first to find the new order intolerable; they were also financially capable of leaving the country, often with significant numbers of followers. The remaining population found itself in a new, direct tenant relationship with the estate owners. The new economic order that these landlords imposed rarely attempted to integrate the tenant population into the overall Scottish economy, and never succeeded in doing so in more than a marginal way. Commercial cultivation was not contemplated, pastoral organization excluded the bulk of the population, and the kelp industry provided only a temporary respite from chronic cash shortages. When the other "solutions" to Highland destitution (namely, the increasingly ubiquitous potato cultivation and cash wages from the fishing industry) failed, as they did in the late 1840s and the early 1880s, the tenant populations were again brought face-to-face with the threat of starvation.[2]

The mid-century crisis had been dealt with by means of private philanthropy and a combination of voluntary and enforced emigration. The crisis of the 1880s did not readily admit of this traditional treatment. A century's erosion of respect for the landlords, the example of the rebellious Irish tenantry, and the emergence of the Highland Land Law Reform Association (HLLRA) all contributed to an atmosphere that demanded a domestic prevention of destitution rather than a further depopulation. The demand of the people was for more land, for the enlargement of existing agricultural holdings, and for the return of land previously cleared of human population for the purposes of sheep and deer. From 1882, when a force of Glasgow constabulary was humiliated at the Battle of the Braes, until the improvement of economic conditions after 1888, the Highlands, and especially, the Western Isles witnessed a constant series of rent strikes, deforcements, and invasions of deer forests that came to be known as the Crofters' War.[3] A general breakdown of law and order was perceived to be occurring. HLLRA membership reached 15,000 in the Highlands by 1885 and, enfranchised for the first time in that year, the crofter and cottar population expressed its political will in the return of four "Crofter MPs" from the Highland constituencies. Particularly in London and Edinburgh, active HLLRA chapters drew constant attention to the Highland land issues. The problem of Highland discontent would not simply go away and government was forced to seek a solution.

The response of the Gladstone government was to appoint a commission, in March 1883, to enquire into social conditions in the Highlands and Islands and to make recommendations for the improvement of those conditions.[4] Under the chairmanship of Baron Napier, the Commission organized quickly and began its first hearing at the Braes in Skye on 8 May. By the time the hearings concluded in Edinburgh in late October, the Commission had held seventy-one meetings in sixty-one locations and had heard evidence from 775 witnesses. It won the confidence of the crofter population by demonstrating that it would tolerate no persecution of witnesses by landlords as a consequence of evidence given. Especially in the Western Isles, expectations were high that the government would enact legislation to benefit the tenant population.

These hopes were severely dampened by the public and parliamentary reception given to the Napier Commission report when it was presented on 28 April 1884. The report was unable to offer a focussed proposal to deal with what was a diffuse problem, and was marred by three separate dissenting opinions on its main recommendations. Avoiding radical solutions such as the cancellation of deer forests and the redistribution of land, the report proposed that a variety of measures be taken, ranging from the creation of townships to public expenditure on piers and communications to security of tenure for those paying in excess of £6 annually in rent.

Noting that a willingness to emigrate had existed in the past amongst Highlanders and arguing that the then current opposition to the idea was not "an ineradicable sentiment," the report recommended that "the last of remedial measures" should be a scheme of state-supported family emigration from the overcrowded crofting districts. Napier cited the Canadian *Dominion Lands Act* and the "success" of the seven families sent to the North-West Territories by Lady Gordon Cathcart from Benbecula in the summer of 1883 as evidence of what could be achieved by willing emigrants. The Napier commissioners contacted colonial dependencies in the southern hemisphere to enquire whether similar arrangements could be made. Commissioner Charles Fraser-Mackintosh dissented from this recommendation in general, but did acknowledge that such a scheme could be justified in relief of the congested population of the Lews and other minor Hebridean islands. As applied to those locations, therefore, the proposal had the unanimous support of the Commission.

Though the commissioners struggled with working definitions of the classes with which they were concerned, the results of their efforts are approved of still by James Hunter, the crofting community's most eminent historian. Acknowledging that the distinction between crofters and cottars was "more easily felt and understood than delineated," the report nevertheless defined the two groups thus:

> By the word crofter is usually understood a small tenant of
> land with or without a lease, who finds in the cultivation and
> produce of his holding a material portion of his occupation,
> earnings and sustenance, and who pays rent directly to the
> proprietor.

> The term cottar commonly imports the occupier of a dwelling
> with or without some small portion of land, whose main
> subsistence is by the wages of labour, and whose rent, if any is
> paid to a tenant and not to the landlord.[5]

Particularly as a description of the small crofter, the emphasis on agricultural occupation was questionable. As early as 1851, one concerned commentator noted that it was inappropriate to regard the crofters

> as a class of small farmers who get ... their living, and ... pay
> rent from the produce of their crofts. They are truly labourers,
> living chiefly by the wages of labour, and holding crofts or lots
> for which they pay rent, not from the produce of the land, but
> from wages.[6]

The categorization of the crofters as cultivators would subsequently be used to advantage by emigrationists to coincide with Canada's proclaimed preference for British agriculturalists.

By the 1880s the numbers of small crofters had increased substantially, particularly on Lewis, where they were no longer distinguishable from the cottars. Moreover, especially with regards to the Western Isles, the definitions of the Napier Commission's report failed to identify the particular nature of the labour through which cottars and small crofters gained their livelihoods. That labour was in the fishing industry. Barra and Lewis were the heart of the annual herring fishery which employed the majority of the male population and, ashore, a significant portion of the female workforce, during its short season from mid-May to late June. Many small crofters and cottars also took part, on boats owned by east coast fishermen, in the North Sea fishing during July and August. In 1890, the Walpole Commission toured the Highlands and Islands taking evidence on the question of state support to the fisheries as a solution to prevailing destitution. The Poor Law officer who had submitted the 1886 confidential reports quoted at the opening of this chapter was a member of that Commission. He was certainly under no illusions about which economic activity sustained the crofter and cottar populations. Elsewhere he wrote, "the herring fishery is the main source of wages open to the great majority of the inhabitants of Skye and the Long Island."[7]

The Napier Commission report did acknowledge, however, that the fishing population was "largely intermixed and identified with the farming class" and that by far the majority of both crofters and cottars were "wholly or largely dependent" for their subsistence on their earnings as fishermen. In urging state intervention on their behalf as a "special case," the first argument the Commission advanced was their importance in the fishing industry, and the second was their utility for naval defence. However, because fishing was not practiced methodically or exclusively by either crofters or cottars, the Commission believed it "must regard the mass of the people as small agricultural tenants," and shaped its definitions to reflect that belief. The definitions accorded well with the aspirations of the crofters and cottars and with the program of the emerging Land League, and were influential in the subsequent legislation enacted to secure and enlarge agricultural holdings. However, the Duke of Argyll, highly critical of Napier for viewing the crofters as a farming class, wrote that this mistake was "the parent of a thousand other mistakes on every other aspect of the question."[8] The Canadian settlements that would be established in 1888 and 1889 can legitimately be viewed as offspring of this "parent."

The response of the British Empire's colonies to the Napier Commission's recommendation on emigration was immediate. Even before the report's presentation to Parliament, Australia responded informally to the enquiries regarding possible crofter settlement, and Cape Colony was said to be considering a scheme specifically for Skye crofters. The Canadian government briefly appointed immigration agents, in September 1884 and July 1885, to promote crofter emigration. It advised the first of these not to render himself "liable to the reproach of having misled" and not to encourage emigration of "the pauper class."[9] The most concrete proposal was received by the Colonial Office from the government of New Zealand by December 1884. The New Zealand legislature authorized the Governor in Council to set aside 10,000 acres on the coast of the North Island between Catlin's River and Mataura as "a special settlement, to be offered to such of the crofters … as may be disposed to emigrate to New Zealand; one-third of such land to be free-granted, in areas not exceeding 10 acres for each adult male." Although the proposal did receive Cabinet consideration, action was not taken owing to the introduction in the British Parliament of crofting legislation in 1885 and again in 1886.

The last enactment of Gladstone's short-lived third administration, the *Crofter Holdings (Scotland) Act* was the reluctant and belated Liberal response to the recommendations of the Napier Commission's report. Aware of its dependence upon the support of the Crofter MPs, and ever mindful of Ireland, Gladstone's administration framed its response to the continuing discontent in the Highlands in terms of land reform, though not along the lines advocated by Napier. Whereas Napier recommended measures to assist the increasing cottar population and security of tenure only for those crofters paying rent in excess of £6 annually, no reference was made in the *Crofter Holdings (Scotland) Act* to the cottars, and crofters paying any rent whatsoever were accorded a statutory security of tenure. A Crofters Commission was established to tour the Highlands and Islands on an ongoing basis, in order to determine the fairness of rents and to adjust those rents where necessary. Although hostile to the *Act* itself, the Crofter MPs were cognizant that, for the first time, the crofting community had received legal recognition of its "special case" status and that the instincts of a Liberal administration were to base its consideration of a response to Highland problems, if not on land redistribution, at least on questions relating to land tenure.

As predicted by those who criticized the *Act* for doing too little too slowly, events in the Highlands would not wait upon long-term outcomes. The geographic focus of Highland discontent in 1887 became the island of Lewis, the only part of the Highlands that had not shared in the general depopulation since the 1850s. In fact, the population of Lewis was still increasing and, according to the census figures of 1886, had risen to 27,000. The serious decline of income from traditional fishing occupations was continuing and the response of both the crofter and cottar populations to the scarcity of provisions was again to demand increased agricultural holdings. This demand found expression in a highly publicized raid on the Park Deer Forest in November. Forcefully making a political point on land use, the raiders also secured a short-term food supply by slaughtering a limited number of deer. A meeting of concerned Stornaway residents petitioned the Secretary for Scotland to conduct an inquiry into conditions on the island. Lord Lothian, the new Secretary for Scotland, acted quickly in appointing Malcolm McNeill, Visiting and Inspecting Officer for the Western Highlands and Islands for the Edinburgh Board of Supervision and author of the confidential reports of 1886, to conduct the inquiry.

MALCOLM McNEILL AND THE "LOTHIAN SCHEME"

Malcolm McNeill had become the Poor Law Inspector in the Western Isles for the Edinburgh Board of Supervision in 1867. His views on the necessity of massive emigration from the Highlands did not differ from those of his employer or those of his uncle, who had urged the Edinburgh Board to adopt a policy of depopulation as early as 1851. For twenty-five years, until 1892, McNeill developed a familiarity with the crofting parishes that few in official circles could equal. That familiarity resulted in considerable influence with the tenant population. After others had failed, it was McNeill who was able to persuade the Glendale fugitives to surrender to authorities in February 1883.[10] This success impressed the Gladstone government, and McNeill was selected in late February as secretary to the Napier Commission, which was appointed in 1883 to investigate the grievances that had resulted in the outbreak of the Crofters' War. As secretary, McNeill apparently heard nothing from the Commission's 775 witnesses to convince him that depopulation had any rival as the only "effectual and permanent" remedy for Highland ills. Returning to his duties with the Board of Supervision upon the conclusion of the Commission's work, he proceeded to recommend the assisted emigration to Australia of the entire population of the island of St. Kilda.[11]

In October 1886, the Secretary for Scotland, A.J. Balfour, received from Malcolm McNeill four reports on the Western Highlands and Islands. These commissioned, confidential reports assessed economic conditions, detailed estate expenditures, and analyzed the strength of Land League and emigrationist sentiment. While he acknowledged the almost universal aversion of crofters and cottars to the idea of emigration, McNeill stated repeatedly that informed opinion consistently held that emigration alone was capable of significantly reducing the problems of poverty and overpopulation affecting the crofting parishes. He concluded by outlining, in considerable detail, his own thoughts on a scheme of state-assisted emigration from the Western Isles. At the same time, he forwarded to the Lord Advocate a petition Lady Gordon Cathcart had received from twenty-eight of her tenants requesting government assistance in emigrating "to some British colony." As the petition indicated, favourable reports from Lady Cathcart's earlier emigrants were stimulating interest in emigration on Benbecula. It was precisely this stimulation that McNeill sought to imitate on a broader scale. This would not be the last time that McNeill would attempt to influence public policy.[12]

McNeill was invited to expand upon his proposals. In a memorandum dated 3 November 1886, he advised the Scottish Office that the Canadian Northwest would be his choice for settlements because the obligation to repay a government loan could be "readily enforced" under the terms of Canada's *Dominion Lands Act*. He recommended small, supervised settlements of Highlanders located amongst established farmers, with each assisted family to have capital of £100 after purchase of transport, outfits, and stock. He urged that the scheme encompass as many as 30,000 families and that emigrants sail directly to Canada from their home parishes to avoid "socialistic" influences at Glasgow and Greenock. Before the end of the year Sir Charles Tupper, the Canadian High Commissioner in London, advised the Scottish Office that his government would "willingly cooperate in any scheme having for its object the emigration of so desirable a class of settlers as the Scotch crofters."[13] Although he stated the Canadian government could not agree to provide settlement supervisors and would be unable to guarantee the repayment of advances, Tupper emphasized that the money loaned would be "secured upon the land," and noted that assisted passages were available to farmers, farm labourers, and their families.

The enthusiasm of the Canadian government was matched by private interests. The President of the Canadian Pacific Railway, Sir George Stephen, was widely recognized as a promoter of prairie settlement. As early as 1881, he had had discussions with the Secretary of State for Ireland in an unsuccessful attempt to develop a scheme to alleviate Irish population pressure through emigration to the Canadian West. The Scottish Office, therefore, sought his views on the viability of a scheme involving crofter emigrants. He urged that the arrangements for such a scheme should be entrusted not to the Canadian government, but to the private land companies. He recommended in particular the Canada North-West Land Company (CNWL), and assured Balfour that, for a family of six, £120 would "render comfort and independence, within a few years, a matter of certainty."[14]

Both Balfour and his successor, Lord Lothian, were highly interested in the emigrationist solution to Highland ills. Fully aware of the concessions gained by the Irish tenantry through threats to public order and civil disobedience, Conservatives and Unionists alike insisted that property rights outside Ireland should not be similarly eroded. Lothian assumed office as Secretary for Scotland on 11 March 1887 determined that the degree of legal recognition accorded to crofter land rights by Gladstone's *Crofter Holdings Act* of 1886 would not be further extended. He explored all possible avenues to reduce the agitation for land reform that found expression in HLLRA meetings in the cities and in deforcements in the Highlands and Islands. Lothian began to investigate the reorganization of the Poor Law rates in the crofting parishes and to press for financial commitments for fisheries loans, public works schemes, and harbour developments.

However, the emigration scheme proposed by Malcolm McNeill offered a far more dramatic and a far more immediate solution to Highland discontent. Lothian, therefore, pressed forward with the negotiations initiated by Balfour with a number of Canadian land companies. He presented proposals to Cabinet in May and July of 1887. The schemes were rejected because private profit from public funds could not be permitted even by a government willing to consider schemes of state-assisted emigration. In December, the frustrated land companies refused to submit new proposals when invited to do so, and a separate British Columbia proposal to develop its deep-sea fishery through crofter settlement was rejected by the Treasury, again in connection with financial requirements.

These rebuffs could not have come at a worse time for Lothian. In the late autumn of 1887, the invasion of the Park Deer Forest on Lady Matheson's estate on the island of Lewis again focussed public attention on the issues surrounding crofter grievances. A detachment of Royal Scots was immediately dispatched to Stornoway and was joined there on 23 December by a detachment of Royal Marines from Plymouth. With the possibility of further disturbances and the certainty of a highly publicized trial for those accused of the Park Deer Forest invasion, Lothian found himself involved in the type of political crisis he most dreaded. The circumstances that could result in an "Irish solution" to Highland discontent were compounding at precisely the moment when prospects for a state-supported emigration scheme seemed most bleak.

Not surprisingly, Lothian turned to Malcolm McNeill. The only documented meeting of the two men took place in December 1887. Before Christmas, a meeting organized in Glasgow by the Land League in support of the Park Deer Forest invaders had echoed the demand of Stornoway residents for a public inquiry into conditions on the island of Lewis. McNeill was asked to conduct such an inquiry, focussing upon the parish of Lochs, to determine if conditions of destitution were as serious as deputations to the Scottish Office claimed. Lothian requested that "the Inquiry may be commenced and conducted with as little delay and as privately as possible."[15]

The subsequent inquiry was conducted with all due speed, commencing on 9 January and concluding on 19 January 1888. But seldom can an inquiry have been conducted less privately. The anticipation of another major disturbance at Aignish Farm combined with McNeill's commission to attract a number of newspaper correspondents to Stornoway. Rather than minimizing contacts with them, McNeill invited the reporters to accompany him aboard HMS *Jackal* during the course of his inquiries. As a result, *The Scotsman* carried lengthy daily reports on McNeill's meetings in the parishes of Lewis and on the poverty and worsening conditions to be found there. Throughout January, the newspaper editorialized on the evils of the Gladstonian response to Irish lawlessness, lamented the acquittals of the Park Deer Forest raiders, and urged migration and emigration as the only "possible remedy for the present state of things."

If Lothian was seeking a renewed impetus for his stalled proposals on assisted emigration, the report McNeill sent from Stornoway on 21 January would not have disappointed him. The report stated that steadily declining income from the fisheries had occasioned widespread hardship, though destitution was not prevalent at the time of the inquiry. But McNeill also insisted that by the end of March

> the bulk of the population of Lochs and elsewhere will be brought face to face with the necessity of killing their cattle and sheep to sustain life, while those who have no stock must either appeal to the parochial board or starve.

The report referred approvingly to Sir John McNeill's recommendation in his 1851 report concerning the removal of population, and ended with two pages of "emigration extracts" citing the need for population reduction and state-aided emigration. The report clearly did not confine itself to description; it was an undisguised attempt to guide policy.[16]

Neither did McNeill restrict himself to report writing. Many minor disturbances also occurred during the tense period of McNeill's inquiry, and several delegations of crofters and cottars met with Lady Matheson, the island's major landowner, urging her to redistribute the land. It was to one of these delegations that she uttered her famous statement: "These lands are mine and you have nothing to do with them." A delegation of men from Back (on Lady Matheson's estate) received only perfunctory encouragement from McNeill when they asked him on 20 January about emigration to British Columbia. On 24 January, when they enquired about emigration to Manitoba, McNeill advised them of Scottish Office plans, helped the petitioners draft a submission to Lothian, and took the petition with him when he left Lewis that evening. Back in Edinburgh, he advised the Board of Supervision that, due to the scarcity of money, the Poor Law structure at Stornoway was in danger of collapse. The Board duly advised Lothian of this on 8 February.

The orchestrated campaign succeeded admirably. After the report was presented to Parliament on 10 February, pro-emigrationist newspapers urged the implementation of an emigration policy, and McNeill himself was requested to accompany the Under Secretary for Scotland on 20 February to a Cabinet subcommittee meeting attended by three senior Ministers: W.H. Smith, the Government House Leader; A.J. Balfour; and J.G. Goschen, the Chancellor of the Exchequer. New proposals were received from Canadian land companies, the long-standing promise of cooperation by the Canadian government was assumed to be secured, and by 7 April, the Treasury had approved the experiment in state-aided emigration and colonization that McNeill had so long and so forcefully advocated. The scheme made a government vote of £10,000, at W.H. Smith's insistence, dependent upon the raising of £2,000 through private subscription. It required the close cooperation of the Canadian authorities, the establishment of an administrative Imperial Colonisation Board (ICB), and the "gratuitous cooperation" of the Canadian land companies. The approval of the scheme surprised the national emigrationist lobby (which was on the verge of presenting its own mature proposal to government) and delighted the Highland landlords, the majority of whom petitioned Lothian for just such a scheme in the spring of 1888.

The scheme approved so abruptly in April 1888 was both a curious and a cumbersome one. The government apparently saw in the rural and "special case" status of the crofters a convenient means of deflecting the persistent demands for state involvement in schemes of urban emigration. A resolution of the financial difficulties with the land companies had certainly not been achieved. However, at this critical moment, Lothian was able to present to Cabinet a memorial signed by most Highland landowners urging state support for public works and emigration. This unquestionably provided Lothian with the kind of eleventh-hour evidence he needed to impress the government that a desperate situation existed. Fully cognizant of the security provisions afforded by the Canadian *Dominion Lands Act*, the government agreed to advance £10,000 towards a scheme of emigration, on the condition that £2,000 would be raised by private subscription. It agreed to the appointment of a Board of Trustees to administer the scheme and to "collect the installments of capital and interest" from the settlers. The involvement of private philanthropy lent moral legitimacy to the scheme while the possibility that private concerns could profit from public money was apparently eliminated by the promise of "gratuitous co-operation" that had been received from the Canadian Pacific Railway Company, the Hudson's Bay Company and the Canada North-West Land Company. The Canadian government undertook to "render every assistance ... in connection with the selection of the land for the emigrants, and their preliminary settlement," and required only that it formally approve of the selected emigrants.[17]

The entire focus of the negotiations conducted by the Scottish Office during the preceding sixteen-month period had been with the land companies, not with the Canadian government. The Canadian High Commissioner, Sir Charles Tupper, advised the Scottish Office in May 1887 that the expenses involved in the mortgage registration could be charged against the homestead, and Tupper did forward the July scheme to his government in August 1887. However, no formal or informal communication occurred between Canadian authorities and the Scottish Office between 8 August 1887 and 10 April 1888. The absence of Sir Charles Tupper from his duties as High Commissioner for most of 1887 and 1888 cannot, by itself, account for the curious failure of the Scottish officials to request information regarding legalities and details of settlement from the Canadian government. At the instigation of a suddenly frantic Scottish Office, questions and directions demanding urgent attention were directed almost daily to Canadian authorities by the Colonial Office after 11 April. Having announced his intention to proceed with the emigration that spring, Lothian sought the official sanction of the British Treasury and the Canadian government. The Colonial Office was requested to urge Canadian acceptance of the scheme and in its letter to Lord Lansdowne, Governor-General of Canada, stated

> that no pecuniary liability will attach to the Canadian Government, and that the duty of collecting the installments of capital and interest will rest on the proposed Board and not on the Dominion officers.

Legislation that would "constitute the Board a corporation capable of suing and being sued" was also requested.[18]

Treasury approval was given on 12 April, but the Canadian reply to the Colonial Office request was not received until 26 April. It promised Canadian cooperation in the "manner suggested," but asked for clarification of the nature of the legislation required. The Scottish Office conferred with the Lord Advocate, but quickly realized that negotiations between Canada and the Colonial Office would require some considerable time. On 28 April, the Scottish Office wrote to the Treasury begging that the scheme's "ratification by Act, warrant, or otherwise" be accomplished by the British government to avoid a further delay. The letter further noted that if the work of selecting the emigrants were not begun immediately, the scheme would of necessity have to be abandoned "until next year."

Lothian was not prepared to wait "until next year." With legalities unclear, with questions of finance unresolved, with less than £700 raised by private subscription, with only the simple assent of a confused Canadian government, and with negotiations with the various land companies still incomplete, the Scottish Office launched its single-minded plan calculated to bring peace to the island of Lewis. Ignoring the respectfully expressed concerns of the Board of Supervision in Edinburgh that a Poor Law officer may "not be in the most favourable position either to select or to persuade emigrants," verbal instructions were given to Malcolm McNeill on 3 May to leave at once for Stornoway.

CHAPTER TWO

Departures

T HE SCHEME approved so unexpectedly in April 1888 was sustained by no practical arrangements whatsoever. The cooperation of the Canadian government had been promised, but beyond the confirmed land grant, the form of that cooperation had not been discussed. Though efforts were being made, no agreement had been reached between the Scottish Office and a settlement company. To implement the emigration experiment, Lothian selected the man whose energy and idealism had first persuaded him that the Highland land problem could be solved. With only general instructions, Malcolm McNeill would be obliged to improvise details of both policy and practice. In a number of significant areas, controversy was to emerge between the emigrants and the scheme's originators as to what had and what had not been promised. Until the settlers were in Canada, the extremely short interval between government sanction and emigrant departures concealed from all concerned the contradictory expectations that had been created.

A series of delays on both sides of the Atlantic prevented the appointment of the administrative board until late December. Until then, the Scottish Office, though reluctant to set policy on behalf of the anticipated board, dealt with the issues arising from the settlement of the first two groups of emigrants. From its appointment at least until its fourth meeting in July 1889, the Imperial Colonisation Board (ICB) attempted only to implement and to supervise decisions taken before it had been constituted and for which it was suddenly responsible. Both the settlers and the scheme's administrators would be obligated for two decades to operate within the framework that evolved so rapidly during the spring and summer of 1888. In order to understand the subsequent relationship between settlers and administrators, a thorough examination of that framework's evolution is necessary.

THE INSTANT EMIGRANTS OF 1888

The island of Lewis was not in a state of turmoil when McNeill arrived in May of 1888. An unusually prosperous spring fishery and the continued presence of sixty marines at Stornoway had combined to end the series of serious land raids initiated by the Park Deer Forest invasion of the previous November. However, the acquittal of the Park Deer

Forest raiders by an Edinburgh jury and the severe sentences sub-sequently given to those arrested during another disturbance at Aignish in January enhanced the uncertainty on the island with regard to both the government's intentions and the Land League's tactics. A nervous Scottish Office was relieved that the imminent opening of the herring fishery was about to provide cash income for the majority of the Lewis population, but recognized that the social and political conditions that led Lothian daily to expect the occurrence of fresh disorder were un-changed. It recognized the numerically increasing cottar population concurred with the crofters that landlessness was the cause of distress, and that both cottars and crofters were willing to act beyond legal re-straint when that condition became severe. Despite Malcolm McNeill's contention that an emigration scheme would be warmly received in the Long Island and despite being in receipt of a considerable number of pro-emigration petitions, the Scottish Office was anxious lest its scheme be thwarted by the proponents of radical land reform. The parliamentary announcement of the scheme on 1 May was restricted to a general out-line of the proposed plan, and no official notice was given, in Parliament or elsewhere, that the Scottish Office had sent an agent to Stornoway for the purpose of selecting families for immediate emigration to Canada.

Malcolm McNeill found himself charged with a major responsibility in the prosecution of the solution to Highland distress that he had so con-sistently advocated. He was instructed to familiarize the people of Lewis with the details of the scheme, to accept preliminary applications for as-sistance to emigrate, and to await the arrival of a representative of the Canadian government, in conjunction with whom he was to select twenty-five families for emigration as soon as was practicable. His serv-ices had been obtained only after the Scottish Office had overruled objections by the Board of Supervision that its employees should not be involved in activities unconnected to their official duties. Though McNeill did not share the reservations expressed by his employer and though he approached his assignment with vigour, he was not without misgivings. Since the scheme was made public in mid-April, the Scottish Office had professed its intention to proceed with the embarkation of a number of families during the emigration season of 1888. This was de-spite a widely shared perception amongst both the plan's critics and proponents that practical difficulties in establishing administrative ma-chinery, in making family selections, and in arranging for departures would prevent the implementation of actual emigration until 1889. McNeill did not accept that these deficiencies were grounds for post-ponement, but he did constantly draw the attention of the Scottish Office to the complications caused by the haste with which he was compelled to act.

McNeill arrived in Stornoway on 5 May without any printed information to circulate amongst the local population. He requested the ministers of the churches to advise their congregations of his presence and to ask those interested in receiving assistance to emigrate to contact him on the morning of Monday, 7 May. The pulpit announcements having been made, McNeill busied himself with the preparation of the dozens of manuscript forms he anticipated he might need, listened to the doubts expressed by local officials whether any applications could be secured on such short notice, and allowed himself the admission that "complete failure" was a possibility. Seed potatoes purchased through a Queensland subscription had arrived, and gutting and kippering crews were already engaged for the approaching herring fishery. McNeill's concern was that the relief these afforded would deflect consideration of emigration as a more permanent solution to distress.

The concerns proved groundless. Over the next three days, McNeill interviewed so many applicant families that he desperately requested an assistant from the Scottish Office. The request was denied and he was able to cope only with the assistance of Sheriff-Substitute Alexander Fraser and a local Poor Law official. Applicants arrived at Stornoway from all parts of Lewis. McNeill several times advised the Scottish Office that 100 families could easily have been obtained.[1] Confident of success, McNeill announced on 7 May that, in order to embark from Glasgow on 19 May, the Lewis emigrants would leave Stornoway the following Monday, 14 May.

Though he heard "on all hands complaints of short notice," McNeill's convictions about family composition prevented the majority of those who embarked on 14 May from having the benefit of even seven days to arrange their affairs. He was firmly convinced of the paramount importance of maximizing the number of potential wage earners and potential farm hands within each family. Even before leaving for Stornoway, he had advised the Scottish Office:

> I don't intend to listen to any applicant with young children;
> looking at the risks of this venture, we must confine ourselves
> to people who will be able to earn wages during next winter,
> otherwise much of the advance will be wasted on subsistence.[2]

Of the fifty families considered by him on 7 May, most were rejected solely on grounds of having young children. Seven families were selected on 7 May and only three more on 8 May. When he received instructions to double that number, McNeill reviewed previously rejected applications and added mature siblings or cousins to reconstitute a "family" and, in several cases, added an unrelated "partner." Though the process resulted in more young children than he would have preferred, the twenty-one families committed to departure when the lists closed on the evening of 10 May included fifty-two males and twenty-eight females over the age of eighteen. Only two were nuclear families.

The time between their dates of acceptance and the date of departure available to the selected families to conclude their affairs on Lewis ranged from four to seven days. It immediately became apparent that arrangements to dispose profitably of personal possessions could not be completed in a few days, and that neighbours and relatives of the prospective emigrants simply did not possess the cash with which to make any purchases. With very little cash of their own, the selected families found themselves unable to generate income to pay their debts to the suddenly insistent merchants of Stornoway. McNeill reported that, prior to the lists closing, several families had withdrawn as a result of this situation and, though others came forward to replace them, the failure of three entire families to embark on 14 May is at least partially attributable to the difficulties encountered in making financial arrangements in such a short time. Eight other adults also failed to embark. The eighteen families who did embark all required cash advances from McNeill that averaged nearly £20 per family. One account, under threat of legal action, was only settled at quayside, delaying the ship's departure. Sixteen families declared £17 in private assets amongst them; the other two families declared £40 and £32. The Lewis families, therefore, left with minimal private cash resources after having expended a considerable portion of their individual £120 advances in settling debts.[3] When he subsequently appeared before the Select Committee on Colonisation, McNeill attributed the need to expend additional government money to provide for their subsistence in Canada entirely to the haste with which the emigrants departed. Yet on 8 May, when the Scottish Office suggested that the departure date be postponed by one week, McNeill responded that the 14 May date must be adhered to, as a change in plan would sow too much "doubt and dissatisfaction."

The Canadian government authorities played only a formal role in the selection process. McNeill had originally expected that a Canadian agent would accompany him to Stornoway on 5 May. Only on 7 May did the Canadian High Commission advise the Scottish Office that it was instructing its Glasgow agent, Thomas Grahame, to proceed to Stornoway as soon as he was advised that the families were "ready for inspection on behalf of the Canadian government." Grahame arrived at Stornoway on the evening of 10 May after the lists had been closed. He accompanied McNeill on the final "tours of inspection" on 11 May, approved of all selections, and left for Glasgow with McNeill and the eighteen families aboard the *Claymore* on 14 May. Canada's formal obligation had been nominally fulfilled. If Canada's priority in 1888 was to accept any potential agriculturalist that Great Britain chose to send, the priorities of the Scottish Office were equally clear. The *Claymore* had barely left Stornoway before Lothian was enquiring about the amount of land released by the emigrants' departure.

Arrangements were made for the families to stay at the Allan Line's Sailors' Home in Glasgow. At the request of the Scottish Office, Gaelic-speaking officers of the district police force met the *Claymore* on the morning of 16 May and plain-clothed officers "guarded" the emigrants until their scheduled departure for Canada aboard the *Corean*.[4] Ostensibly being protected from the "socialistic influences" of Glasgow, the eighteen families were, in fact, being sheltered from exposure to any last-minute efforts by Land League sympathizers to persuade them to return to Lewis. At least one Land League sympathizer was at quayside urging them not to abandon Scotland. Though by no means coerced, the emigrant families were uncertain that their abandonment of Lewis was in their own interests and in the interests of those left behind. Their decision to leave Lewis, though in keeping with the Scottish Office's strategy of easing population pressure on the land and thereby weakening political pressure for land reform, meant the abandonment of both land and principles deeply held. The decision had been spontaneous, necessitous, and anxious.

Evidence is not conclusive, but it appears that the scheme was so rapidly implemented that the Lewis emigrants left Glasgow unaware of their destination. The inability of the land companies and the Scottish Office to agree upon specific terms continued well into May. The newly formed Commercial Colonisation Company of Manitoba was intended by the Scottish Office to act as its Canadian agent, but on 9 May the company's financial requirements were found to be excessive and were forwarded to the Treasury only in anticipation of rejection.[5] However, a working arrangement was developing with the CNWL office in Edinburgh — a development that grew out of Scottish Office enquiries about the arrangements made by that company for the Cathcart emigrants in 1883 and 1884. The minimal extent of the Canadian government's role in the early development of Lothian's scheme is revealed by the fact that McNeill obtained the Canadian Department of Interior's applications for homestead entry from Peacock Edwards, an official of the CNWL in Edinburgh, and not from either the Canadian High Commission in London or the Canadian agent in Glasgow.

An embarrassed but grateful Scottish Office found the CNWL willing to act. As a result, the company was asked to urgently direct its Winnipeg agent to

> select good Government 160 acre sections in Manitoba for Emigrants, to meet them on arrival and to make all other necessary arrangements... Please keep matters as private as possible.[6]

The company cabled its Canadian Commissioner, W.B. Scarth, to that effect on 11 May and advised the Scottish Office that it was mistaken about the sailing date. The *Corean*, understood by both McNeill and the Scottish Office to be embarking on 19 May, was in fact scheduled to leave on 17 May. Scarth first considered the Moosomin area as a possible location, but decided upon the Killarney area upon advice that sufficient good government land was available there. The CNWL received his telegram stating "TS 4 and 5, Range 16, W 1 ... Pelican Lake" on 17 May. Lothian was also relieved to hear from Sir George Stephen that a CPR official and members of the local St. Andrews Society would meet the eighteen Lewis families at Quebec City. Stephen added that his only regret was that the number of families was just eighteen and not eighteen thousand.

By mid-May, the Office of the High Commission in London began to awaken to the implications of the emigration scheme. It suggested to the Scottish Office on 15 May that it was "rather late" in the emigration season to contemplate the dispatch of more settlers, and declared more emphatically on 18 May that there was no time to be lost in making arrangements in Canada. But Lothian was not to be dissuaded. He ordered McNeill to proceed to Harris immediately. Malcolm McNeill and Thomas Grahame arrived in Harris on 19 May to select one dozen families for emigration from Glasgow on 1 June. Local clergy again agreed to make announcements from their pulpits and had done so on 13 May. McNeill and Grahame conducted interviews on Monday, 21 May and by Thursday, 24 May had inspected and approved twelve applications for government assistance to emigrate. The group was to leave Harris on 28 May. To make practical arrangements, therefore, the Harris emigrants had no more time than the Lewis group had — namely, seven days at best. Eleven of the twelve heads of families received cash advances averaging just under £10. Nine families declared no private means, though one family declared £45. The only departures from the Lewis selection process were the involvement of a local philanthropist in recommending nine of the twelve families and her provision of extra clothing for them at no cost. The nine families came from the estate of Lord Dunmore in South Harris; the other three families were from North Harris.

The households selected were subject to the same addition of potential wage earners as the Lewis "families," but the resultant family size was considerably larger. One included the family head's seven brothers and sisters aged between fourteen and twenty-seven; the "head" of the family was thirty years of age. Nine other families included collectively sixteen other brothers, sisters, and relatives. In contrast to the departure from Lewis, no entire family failed to embark when the packet left Harris on 28 May. Two adults refused to go at the last minute and a third was not permitted by McNeill to board the ship when it was learned he would be leaving a destitute father behind. McNeill was seeking a reduction in the rates, not another dependent upon them.[7]

Delighted that the radical newspapers had no local correspondents on Harris, McNeill accompanied the ninety-seven Harris emigrants to Glasgow, arriving on 30 May. They were accommodated at the Home For Scotch Passengers on Broomielaw Street for three days. The sailing of the *Buenos Aryean* had been postponed to 2 June, allowing the Harris emigrants to learn before sailing of Scarth's 1 June decision to locate them close to the Lewis settlers. Whether through benevolence or another attempt to avoid Land League "agents," the Harris men were treated by Thomas Grahame to a tour of the Canadian section at the newly opened Glasgow International Exhibition.

In correspondence with his supervisors at the Scottish Office, McNeill expressed his hopes that the Canadian government would make a "supreme effort" and that it was aware of "the *absolute necessity* of making these first lots a big success." He compared the two groups in a private note. "The Harris men," he wrote, "have hardly such fine physique as those from the Lews but 'per contra' they seem more intelligent, less 'savage', and less 'jammed' cheeky." In making his official report, he declared that, apart from the failure to embark of the three Lewis families, "the first experiment under the Government Colonisation Scheme ... is completed ... without a single unfavourable incident..."[8] He anticipated that a thousand families from Lewis alone would be prepared to emigrant the following spring. Though the experiment had barely begun, McNeill banished any doubts he may have entertained about Canadian commitment to Scottish Office objectives and returned, warmly commended, to his position at the Board of Supervision on 6 June.

A WINTER OF UNCERTAINTIES
Eager to proceed with its mandate, the Scottish Office insisted, only

three months later, that the Board of Supervision grant McNeill another leave of absence. Under instruction to select forty families for emigration to the Canadian Northwest in the spring of 1889, McNeill returned to Stornoway in mid-September. It was the intention of the Scottish Office that the entire process leading to the emigration of 1889 should be conducted in a more efficient and calculated manner. During the selection process in May, McNeill had had no printed information to make available to applicants, and only in Harris was he able to use printed, official application forms. By 3 September, information was available for distribution in both Gaelic and English, and posters in both languages were forwarded to the offices of registrars throughout the Western Isles. The Scottish Office believed that an early selection of families would allow for the sale of goods and chattels, thereby avoiding both the necessity of cash advances in Scotland and the complaints of cash shortages in Canada that formed the only serious complaint emanating from the emigrants of May and June.

The extent of Lothian's commitment to the emigration scheme is revealed in his nervous acquiescence in the withdrawal of the marines from Stornoway on 7 September. The Admiralty would agree to make HMS *Seahorse* available to facilitate McNeill's selection tour only if the marines could return to headquarters in the south of England. Though Lothian feared further outbreaks of disorder and affirmed his right to recall the force when necessary, he agreed. The *Seahorse* was made available on 20 September.

McNeill left Glasgow on 14 September in the company of Thomas Grahame. By the time the emigrant selection process was completed on 5 October, they had received 161 formal applications and claimed to have received an equal number of verbal applications. Stating that 100 suitable families could have been obtained in Lewis alone, McNeill was nevertheless perplexed that a number of ministers had refused to make pulpit announcements and that the promotional posters "were almost instantly torn down throughout the Long Island."[9] The forty families selected, almost without exception, were relatives of the spring emigrants, but were subject to two conditions that had not been previously applied. First, McNeill was instructed not to approve of families whose expenses before arrival in Canada were likely to exceed £50. Second, the Scottish Office determined that no cash advances would be permitted, and it encouraged the application of families with some private means. Evidence suggests, however, that these emigrants were to arrive in Canada with less private resources than did their predecessors, and McNeill later testified that he always selected the poorest families he could obtain. As viewed by McNeill, the scheme was very much a late-Victorian exercise in "shovelling out paupers."

In reporting to the Scottish Office in October, McNeill stated:

> I continue of opinion that, if due care be exercised in selection here and in settlement in the Colony, our tentative efforts surely indicate the least costly and most effective means of restoring peace and contentment to the Western Highlands.[10]

He had considerable grounds for optimism. The political battle outside the Highlands was clearly being won by those favouring emigration as a solution to discontent in the crofting counties. When the Treasury authorized the advance of £3,500 from the Civil Contingencies Fund on 10 May, the Scottish Office proceeded in the belief that the full £10,000 would be approved after Parliamentary formalities. The government delayed bringing the question before Parliament, and the four Crofter MPs were not the only Scottish members enraged that public funds were being spent without parliamentary approval. The government had little difficulty in ignoring the objections raised, largely due to the welcome accorded the scheme by the National Association for Promoting State-Directed Emigration and Colonization, whose many parliamentary members viewed the scheme as the harbinger of a much more considerable government involvement. The Highland landowners were pleased, but publicly silent. Privately, Lady Matheson offered to cable the Canadian Prime Minister, High Commissioner, or anyone else the Scottish Office wanted her to contact in favour of the scheme.

The Highland newspapers joined with Glasgow's *North British Daily Mail* in remaining highly skeptical of the scheme, if not overtly critical. But in September 1888, the Scottish Office and McNeill engaged in a successful manipulation of the Scottish press that effectively silenced all but their most virulent opponents. The newspapers were cordially invited to print an optimistic account of the crofters' prospects at Killarney by a recent visitor to the area, and most major papers willingly complied. The *North British Daily Mail* prefaced the account with its own comment, but only the *Highland News* of Inverness demanded payment before doing so, stating the letter was "distinctly of the character of an advertisement."[11] McNeill procured copies of favourable letters from the Killarney settlers to their relatives in the Long Island and *The Scotsman* published two of these on 21 September, precisely coinciding with McNeill's arrival in Stornoway to make the new selection of emigrants. *The Scotsman* also provided McNeill with 100 printed copies of another letter McNeill himself had received and which he wanted to distribute to prospective applicants during the autumn selection process. The forty families selected responded to the favourable letters sent home by the earlier emigrants precisely as McNeill had predicted they would. With the precedent before them, they sought to join their successful relatives and friends near Killarney; the "magnet" in Manitoba had been created and the expected wave of resultant emigration was beginning to develop. The plan was working perfectly.

Standing in sharp contrast to the rapid family selection process was the slow evolution of an acceptable administrative framework. The scheme authorized on 7 April 1888 called for the creation of a board consisting of appointees representing the British and Canadian governments, the major land companies, and the private donors. A query of the Colonial Office received the reply that no precedent in British experience existed for such a board and the suggestion that all appointments should be made by the respective interests. Recognition of the difficulties that could arise if two board members were Canadian residents resulted in the Scottish Office submitting to the Secretary of State for the Colonies on 1 October the proposal that, *ex officio*, the Secretary for Scotland, the Canadian High Commissioner, and the Lord Provost of Glasgow should be appointed to the board, with Peacock Edwards representing the land companies. But again the Canadian authorities delayed. Unofficially, the High Commission Office intimated on 30 August that Sir Charles Tupper would agree to serve; officially, Tupper did not accept the appointment until 25 October. Significantly, he stated that he accepted only "on the understanding that neither [he] nor the Canadian Government incur any pecuniary liability in consequence of [his] doing so."[12]

The Canadian Governor-General's formal approval of the appointment did not reach the Scottish Office until 10 November 1888. By that date, as a result of numerous accounting disputes with the Scottish Office over the Killarney settlement process, the CNWL had resolved to have nothing more to do with government-assisted crofter emigration and Peacock Edwards's nomination was withdrawn. In addition, the possibility existed that a government-proposed Select Committee on Colonisation could soon result in the cancellation of the entire scheme. Ultimately Tupper was able to persuade Thomas Skinner, a man of various financial interests in London (and incidentally, a director of the CNWL), to sit on the board as representative of the land companies. Skinner accepted on 22 December. The ICB was officially proclaimed on 26 December, and arrangements were made to hold the first meeting on 7 February 1889.

When it met, the ICB faced an agenda severely complicated by political difficulties. The proponents of emigration at the Scottish Office had lost their propaganda advantage in mid-November when Glasgow's

Lord Provost received a petition signed by all eighteen of the Lewis emigrant family heads. The petition alleged that the promise of a year's subsistence had been broken and that, as the advances were all spent, the settlers faced destitution. In a letter to the Scottish Office, McNeill raged against "these ungrateful scoundrels." Both McNeill and Thomas Grahame adamantly denied having made such a promise and, though knowledge of the petition was apparently not made public, the argument that the Highland population would necessarily be better off materially in western Canada had been dealt a serious blow.

Breach of promise would prove to be the major argument the opponents of emigration in Lewis and Harris would use over the course of the winter of 1888-89. The forty families who had been recruited to emigrate in the spring of 1889 shared the extreme misgivings opponents of their departure expressed, and as early as 21 October one prospective emigrant withdrew, stating that his wife was suddenly "out and out opposed" to leaving Lewis; another family was regarded as doubtful by 8 November. Lady Matheson privately advised Lothian that though the inclination to emigrate still prevailed, her tenants were beginning to talk about the severity of Canadian winters. She urged the Scottish Office to extend the scheme to include New Zealand before the uncharacteristic burst of emigration fever ended. The death of one of the Harris emigrants at Pelican Lake in late November added to the sense of uneasiness, and several other families withdrew during the winter. However, private letters from the settlers generally contained "such good encouragement" that applications for assistance to emigrate addressed to McNeill far outnumbered the withdrawals by the end of January 1889. McNeill earlier had advised the Scottish Office that vacancies should not be filled until January because "by that time the 'pinch' [would] begin to be felt and there [would] be no difficulty in selecting." McNeill was certainly familiar with the cruel cycle of scarcity in the Western Isles: new applications were received in late January just as he predicted.

That the replacement selections had not been made by the time the ICB met on 7 February was due to difficulties in securing both the private and the parliamentary funding. The response to the public appeal for £2,000 had been disappointing, and after deductions for printing and advertising, the Lord Provost of Glasgow (who was responsible for the collection) was able to forward to the Scottish Office £1,000 only. This sum was sufficient to justify the parliamentary vote to settle the Pelican Lake crofters, but clearly would not allow for any further emigration. W.H. Smith, First Lord of the Treasury and Government House Leader, advised Lothian that a further parliamentary vote would not be possible until the remainder of the £2,000 private subscription had been raised. Lothian pointedly reminded Smith that the inclusion of a private subscription had been ill-advised in the first place and that he was not himself responsible for proposing that aspect of the scheme. It cannot be stated whether this unresolved dispute resulted in the exclusion of the emigration scheme from the debate on the Scottish Estimates, but when debate ended on 13 December, no further money had been voted for crofter emigration.

At its first meeting, therefore, the ICB faced the possibility of having to withdraw the offer to assist the emigration of the families McNeill had selected in October. Even McNeill was beginning to discourage fresh applicants for assistance to emigrate, advising them that no funds were available. However, Lothian had not been idle. In early December, he had written making a personal appeal to numerous Scottish landowners and had been successful in receiving pledges for at least £700. Sir Charles Tupper urged W.H. Smith to make a quick decision in order to avoid the difficulties associated with the late arrival at Pelican Lake the previous year. Once convinced that the full £2,000 private subscription would be raised, Smith and the Chancellor of the Exchequer decided to agree upon the proposed emigration and so advised the Scottish Office on 23 February.

Arrangements then moved rapidly forward. The estate managers for South Harris and North Uist and the chamberlain of the Lews were advised on 25 February of the names of the families selected from their districts the previous autumn. The Board of Supervision was advised that Malcolm McNeill should start at once for Stornoway, and the ICB's secretary was instructed to make arrangements for a 3 April departure. An offer from the Montreal and Western Land Company to locate the anticipated emigrants near Churchbridge, on the Manitoba and North Western Railway line, was declined because it was too distant from Pelican Lake. Through Edgar Dewdney, the Canadian Minister of the Interior, a Gaelic-speaking agent was appointed at Winnipeg on 1 March and ordered to select sufficient government land for an anticipated forty families.

McNeill initially had little difficulty in filling the places vacated by some of the original families, but he was unable to officially advise those selected that their emigration was a certainty until the parliamentary vote finally occurred on 20 March. He was faced with a new wave of desertions after 15 March when he was informed that the destination of the prospective emigrants was to be Wolseley Station, in the North-West Territories, and not Pelican Lake with their friends and relatives in Manitoba. McNeill's task was not made any easier when Lothian over-ruled his Under-Secretary and insisted that the parliamentary vote did not limit the number of families to forty, but rather that fifty-five families could be emigrated with the funds available.[13]

The ten days between the official confirmation of departure on 20 March and the embarkation from Stornoway were at least as hectic for the 1889 emigrants as the similar period had been for those who departed in 1888. The attempts to settle affairs at such short notice were complicated by the Scottish Office's insistence that, unlike the previous year, no cash advances were to be made. This insistence was entirely due to an opinion expressed by the Canadian Minister of Justice that attempts to secure, on Canadian land, money used to pay Scottish debts would constitute fraud.[14] McNeill's instructions were, for the first time, very precise on this point. He advised the Scottish Office on 26 March that nineteen families had withdrawn over time and that he doubted that all of the fifty-two families then on his lists would embark. This uncertainty was communicated to Canada when, on 25 March, the High Commissioner's Office advised the Winnipeg agent that fifty families could be expected, but that preparation should be made for only forty-five. As late as 29 March, two Harris families withdrew and replacements were found. Of the twenty-six Lewis families selected in the autumn, sixteen had withdrawn. While the Treasury, the Scottish Office, and the Canadian High Commission sought desperately to settle administrative and financial details, forty-six families left Stornoway on 31 March, stopping at North Uist to pick up three more families waiting there. Four men were "accidentally left at Tobermory" but, travelling via Oban, rejoined the party on 3 April in Glasgow, and had the extra travel costs deducted from their advances.

The forty-nine families who left Glasgow aboard the *Scandinavian* on 3 April 1889 were seen off by Malcolm McNeill and the ICB's newly appointed secretary, J.G. Colmer. (Interestingly, McNeill's active role in the scheme ended with the departure of the *Scandinavian*, while Colmer, as ICB secretary and as the permanent secretary to the Canadian High Commission, was just beginning an administrative involvement that would last for two full decades.) In a letter to Lothian, Colmer noted that, unlike the 1888 emigrants, the 1889 group had "avoided the disagreeable necessity, and expense, of their spending a day or two about Glasgow." He noted that one man's anxiety at leaving was calmed only by promising him that a Gaelic Bible would be brought aboard at Greenock where the medical inspection was to take place. Colmer was impressed that the funds available in Canada to the Wolseley crofters would be nearly £85 per family, £18.10 more than the money available to the Pelican Lake families. He did not mention that thirty-three family heads had declared no private resources whatsoever and that only three took with them assets of over £10. Though the average family size was considerably lower than that of the 1888 group, the 1889 emigrants were markedly poorer than their predecessors. The twenty-nine families selected in March declared only £48 amongst them. Colmer noted that "the very satisfactory tone" of letters from the Pelican Lake settlers had carried the day against the scheme's opponents and concluded that with "ordinary industry, energy and perseverance" the emigrants were bound to succeed at Wolseley where land had already "been secured for them."[15]

The forty-nine families were not yet at Halifax when the British government ordered the appointment of a select committee to assess the colonization scheme it had so reluctantly sanctioned. The twenty-one-member Select Committee on Colonisation was appointed on 12 April 1889. It was comprised of members holding widely divergent views on the principle of state aid for emigration, and included members of the National Association for Promoting State-Directed Emigration and Colonization as well as Dr. G.B. Clark, the Lothian scheme's harshest parliamentary critic. The emigrationist lobby saw the Committee as an indication that the government was moving towards involvement in emigration and anticipated a strong endorsement of its views. The Committee's mandate was to look at various schemes of colonization, but the government's clear intention, in addition to subjecting all such schemes to close scrutiny, was to postpone any further commitment to the crofter colonization venture. All plans for state-assisted emigration were required to wait upon the Committee's report, but the only practical, large-scale scheme the Committee could examine was Lothian's "experiment" with crofter settlements on the Canadian Prairies. The fate not only of the crofter scheme, but of all schemes of state-aided emigration, therefore, was dependent upon the progress of the 475 people so hurriedly dispatched from the Western Isles in 1888 and 1889.

CHAPTER THREE

Arrivals

T HE ARRIVAL in Canada of the seventy-nine crofter families in 1888 and 1889 presents a complicated mix of personalities and events that must be discussed at considerable length in order to understand the subsequent administration and history of the settlements. To a very great extent, the difficulties experienced at Killarney and later at the settlement established near Saltcoats, though often not identical, were the logical outcomes of an emigration scheme that was flawed in conception and rushed in implementation. The families who came to Canada under Lothian's scheme all left Scotland with only the most preliminary preparation having been made to receive them. These arrangements were modified at considerable expense, but with some success, at Killarney; settlement at Saltcoats was achieved more economically, but less successfully. At both locations, land companies provided the direction and supervision required; at Saltcoats, the Department of the Interior assisted in the settlement process almost against its will. Because the settlement scheme was quite literally a "calculated risk," this chapter must examine, to some extent, the origins of the tedious financial calculations that would occupy administrators, merchants, and land companies for years to follow. The Scottish Office and the ICB controlled only the purse strings and appeared to be helpless witnesses to events and developments beyond their control until the late summer of 1889. At that time, the Canadian government insisted that the crofter settlements were entirely an Imperial responsibility. Belatedly, the ICB turned to consider the creation of an administrative framework.

SETTLEMENTS AT PELICAN LAKE

When the CNWL's office in Winnipeg received instructions to select government land for twenty-one crofter families, the request would have been regarded as almost routine. Previous to 1888, three separate parties from the Western Isles had been settled at Wapella, Moosomin, and Regina. The Orkney-born Winnipeg director of the CNWL, W.B. Scarth, had been personally involved on all three occasions. Scarth had been a fundraiser for the Conservative party in Ontario, had come to Manitoba reluctantly at the request of Sir John A. Macdonald, and was Conservative MP for Winnipeg at the time of the crofters' arrival. He initially considered Moosomin as the location for the anticipated twenty-one

27

Lewis families, but found that a sufficient quantity of government land was not available there. The Canadian government, at Colmer's request, instructed its Commissioner of Dominion Lands at Winnipeg, Henry Hall Smith, to act in conjunction with Scarth to settle the crofters. The decision was taken to settle the Lewis families at Pelican Lake in southwestern Manitoba and, on 19 May 1888, a private rail car containing Scarth and other officials was left at Killarney, the village closest to the proposed settlement location.[1]

The Canadian government made 150 homestead locations available at Pelican Lake for crofter settlement. Upon inspection, however, Scarth considered that only five of these were fit for settlement. In a move that was later to be criticized by other directors of the CNWL, Scarth decided that the shortage of time would not permit the inspection of government land in another locality and made arrangements to settle the immigrants on his own company's lands near Pelican Lake. Before the eighteen Lewis families arrived at Killarney, Scarth received the written assurance of Prime Minister Sir John A. Macdonald that the CNWL would receive equivalent government lands elsewhere as compensation.[2]

On 1 June, the ninety-eight Lewis emigrants arrived at Quebec City where they were regarded by the immigration agent as having been "brought to Canada under the auspices of charitable societies and individuals." As promised by Sir George Stephen, they were met by members of Quebec City's St. Andrew's Society, given food and advice, and then departed immediately for Manitoba. The party arrived at Killarney on 4 June and began the process of selecting homestead sites. Fragmentary evidence suggests that, although some settlers were initially dissatisfied with their locations, the crofters left the village of Killarney for their respective locations one week later, after a selection process that had been amicable and which had been conducted in an atmosphere of cooperation. Selections were made by Scarth "in conjunction with a committee of the representative men among the crofters," and locations apparently were not forced upon any individual against his will. The homesteads were located in Townships 4 and 5 of Ranges 16 and 17, west of the prime meridian, between Killarney and Pelican Lake.

Houses were being erected with the assistance of local tradesmen, and potatoes had already been sown on rented land by the time the ninety-five Harris emigrants arrived at Killarney on 17 June. The *Manitoba Free Press* reported that the new arrivals were enjoying a sandy beach on Pelican Lake and were to be located on Townships 5 and 6 of Ranges 15 and 16, northeast of Pelican Lake in the District of Argyle. (Hereafter, when considered separately, the emigrants will be identified either by their place of origin in Scotland or by their Canadian settlement location. Hence the Lewis party often will be referred to as the Killarney settlers, and the Harris party as the Argyle settlers. When considered together, they will be referred to as the Pelican Lake settlers.) The process of homestead selection proceeded less smoothly with the Harris arrivals. Apparently, without advising Scarth, one father and son exchanged their locations, and three of the twelve family heads simply squatted on sites they desired, in two instances displacing younger men. But Dominion Day activities organized by Scarth and his officials were enjoyed by all, provided a celebration of their prospects in Manitoba, and symbolized the spirit of cautious optimism that was beginning to prevail amongst both Lewis and Harris settlers.

If the settlers concurred with the opinions of Malcolm McNeill and the Scottish Office that this well-considered scheme of settlement could only succeed, officials of the CNWL on both sides of the Atlantic were rapidly developing a less optimistic viewpoint. The establishment of effective communications proved a serious difficulty. Both the Scottish Office and the CNWL were determined to minimize costs and therefore were inclined to cable brief messages that often confused as much as they informed their recipients. Authority for the settlement scheme rested with the Scottish Office in London. Instructions emanated from there, were conveyed to the CNWL's Edinburgh office, and were transmitted thence to the independent-minded Scarth, who did not hesitate to express his opinions when he felt those instructions were inadequate.

As the CNWL was acting as the business agent in Canada for the Scottish Office, it was with reference to financial arrangements that Scarth increasingly expressed his concern. The hasty implementation of the scheme in the United Kingdom meant that the Scottish Office had no practical plans to meet the financial requirements of settlement in Canada. On 29 May, before the arrival of the first group, it was agreed that Scarth would advance money to the settlers and make all necessary expenditures; he would then debit the land company's Edinburgh office which in turn would bill the Scottish Office. But the records of expenditures made by McNeill in Scotland had been surrendered by the *Corean's* captain to the immigration officer at Quebec City. Scarth, therefore, made these Canadian expenditures completely unaware of the extent of the Scottish advances to each family head. When he finally managed to obtain the statements on 14 June, the purchase of materials, implements, and livestock for the Lewis settlers was well advanced, and the Harris group was nearly at Winnipeg.

As individuals involved not only with crofter colonization, but with

Western settlement in general, both Scarth and Edwards were appalled at what those statements revealed. As a result of his experience with the Cathcart crofter settlers, Scarth had stated repeatedly that crofter colonists required "at the very least £100 on their arrival at their destination." Instead he found that the average sum remaining to the Lewis families was less than £69. (The rate of exchange in 1888 was just under five Canadian dollars to one pound sterling. Therefore, £120 was worth nearly $600 Canadian. This rate of exchange remained remarkably stable for the duration of the settlement scheme.) High travel costs due to large family size and deductions used to pay outstanding debts on Lewis had seriously eroded the capital intended for settlement and farm-making purposes. With a credit of just over £86, John Mackay's small nuclear family came closest to satisfying Scarth's financial expectations; with less than £50 to their credit, John Nicolson's party of four fell far short of possessing sufficient funds "to be properly settled." Scarth realized that the Scottish Office retained unexpended funds as a result of the refusal of three families to leave Lewis. On 14 June, he cabled Edinburgh seeking permission to "divide £360 for the three families who did not embark among unmarried homesteaders taking usual security." Edwards realized that this was a departure from the scheme approved by the Treasury, but reminded the Scottish Office of the political reality that it was "of the utmost importance at the start that these pioneer settlers should have sufficient to establish them under conditions likely to ensure their success."[3] This was an argument with which Lothian certainly agreed. He promptly obtained the agreement of the Exchequer, and Scarth was notified by 22 June 1888.

By that date, Scarth was in possession of the financial statements of the Harris emigrants and found their situation even more serious. The average sum available to the family heads was less than £63. Three of the twelve had less than £50 remaining to their credit and one of them, Donald Mackinnon, had less than £35. Scarth advised Edwards that it was impossible to arrange settlement under the circumstances and suggested that all males over eighteen be given homestead locations, with liens held by either the British government or the CNWL. The maximum lien that legally could be taken on a single quarter section had been raised by Canadian statute in 1886 to $600, very nearly the equivalent of £120. Scarth was not overstating his case when he argued that it was "impossible" to settle families who had just over half that amount available. His plan was first, to transfer to the other family members a portion of the debt incurred by family heads prior to their arrival in Killarney, and second, to secure that portion by taking liens on homesteads granted to those relatives and partners. Further expenditure to establish the family heads' farms would then be allowable under the *Dominion Lands Act* up to the $600 maximum.

Both measures required more money. On 23 June, Scarth advised Edwards that $4,000 extra would be necessary to settle the crofters adequately. Edwards responded that no more money was possible, expressed reservations about granting homesteads to the younger men, and advised Scarth to concentrate on the establishment of the family heads' homesteads. Scarth cabled tersely: "In that case must make some settlers return oxen and waggons, increasing agitation." Scarth later explained that he meant such action on his part would result in increasing agitation in the Highlands. The more immediate agitation created at the Scottish Office by this cable resulted in a meeting between Edwards and Lothian and a promise to commit a further £360 to the Manitoba settlers. Financial demands continued to escalate. On 22 July, Scarth advised his startled Edinburgh office that he must have "at least extra fourteen hundred pounds." When pressed for a full explanation, he cabled: "Have written fully. Impossible to explain by cable. Fault entirely your side Atlantic."[4]

Much of the difficulty experienced by Scarth is certainly attributable both to the speed with which the scheme was implemented and to the inadequate analysis of the costs of transportation from Lewis to Killarney and of farm establishment in Manitoba. Significantly absent from the Scottish Office's preparations was any critical examination of statements that £100 to £120 would prove sufficient. Until the scheme was under way, no one expressed the concern that United Kingdom expenditures could jeopardize the success of the Canadian colony. The Scottish Office, with the fiscally orthodox Treasury looking over its shoulder, thought exclusively in terms of sums that could be secured, not of sums that might be required. A second aspect inadequately addressed by Lothian was the strategy which family units were intended to adopt in Manitoba. McNeill had inflated both "family" size and travel costs by adding extra adults to most nuclear families. His avowed intention was to create functional economic units that would allow for farm establishment as well as outside work for wages. Yet, at the same time, he clearly intended that each male over eighteen years of age should be granted a homestead and sent Scarth precisely the correct number of homestead applications required for that purpose. Scarth advised Edwards that the young men from both Lewis and Harris all maintained that they had been promised homesteads before they left Scotland. Two or more homesteads per "family" certainly had the effect of dividing the labour and financial resources of the family. Edwards and the Scottish Office were surprised that homesteads for younger males were even contemplated; McNeill and Scarth assumed they were part of the scheme.

Scarth's cryptic cables caused much consternation in the Scottish Office during May and June, but ultimately there was little choice but to trust the judgement of the "man on the spot." By the time he returned to Winnipeg on 22 July, the financial structures he had suggested were in place. Each of the family heads was settled on a homestead, and all but three were secured by liens for the Canadian equivalent of the full £120. The largest settlement costs were incurred in the purchase of oxen ($120 to $130), cows ($37), wagons ($67.50) and ploughs ($22.50). It seems that Scarth minimized the settlement costs in several ways: first, by virtue of bulk buying, the settlers were supplied with some materials at rates cheaper than those then prevailing in the district; second, there is evidence that Scarth convinced the CPR to charge only half the usual freight rate; and third, there is no record of carpenters' charges for the construction of the settlers' houses.[5]

At the same time, local merchants and hoteliers certainly enjoyed a prosperous summer. Killarney merchant T.J. Lawlor provided the initial evening meals consisting of biscuits, corned beef, oysters, salmon, peaches, plums, and tea at a total cost of over $25. The crofters' first breakfast in Killarney was also provided by Lawlor at a cost of $1.42 per family. James McCann received over $75 for meals for "the Harris batch." W. Cooney charged $60 for teaming the Harris settlers to their homesteads, while W. Pritchard charged $30 for rental of a hall for their shelter. Alexander Gouldie charged over $150 for providing meals for the Lewis settlers and for room and board at his Killarney hotel for Scarth, his wife, and land company officials. Including cables, rail fares, and supplies, over $1,000 was thus expended in "settlement costs," more than half of which was charged to the thirty family heads.[6]

The willingness of the other family members to have the excess debt of the family heads secured against their own homestead entries ensured that Scarth was not obliged to repossess oxen or wagons. Thirty-eight individuals, including a widow of 50 years of age, two males over 60 and, illegally, three males under 18, thereby had £504 charged amongst them.[7] Donald Mackinnon, for example, as the head of a family of ten, had seen much of his initial advance committed to travel expenses. When settlement costs were added, Mackinnon faced a debt of $850. His mother and brother assumed responsibility for the amount over the $600 limit set by the *Dominion Lands Act*, and Mackinnon was able to retain his ox and his wagon. Most individual debts ranged from $50 to $200, well below what Scarth regarded as the market value of their quarter sections, which he put at $4 per acre. No livestock or material were provided to these other family members, and no houses were built for them. Before leaving Killarney, Scarth had taken leins from only eight of the thirty-eight, as most of the young men were away at work by mid-July.

The advantages of locating the crofters in a settled area were well demonstrated in the summer of 1888. Bumper crops were expected and wages were high. A survey conducted at Tupper's request by a Dominion Lands official in September reported that forty of the homesteaders were "out at service" or "working for wages." A few daughters were also reported to be earning wages. The Lewis settlers communally were able to rent a potato field from a neighbouring established settler. They expressed contentment that Presbyterian churches were in their localities and only regretted that a Gaelic-speaking minister or teacher was not in residence. Letters sent to Scotland, and the Dominion Lands report, fully supported Scarth's declaration that he left well-satisfied and contented crofter settlements near Pelican Lake. Optimism was so high that one Lewis settler wrote to the *Glasgow Herald* and spoke of sending gold home soon. Scarth was confident that he had fulfilled his instructions not to locate the crofters too closely together and assured Edwards:

> there is no risk of combination for political or other purposes, as the Crofters are well interspersed with good Canadian Farmers and are anything but in a body, as they extend over a district 20 miles in length and by 12 miles in breadth.[8]

One issue, however, remained unresolved and was to result in precisely the type of political combination the Scottish Office most hoped to avoid. That issue was the question of how the nearly 200 people were to be provided for during their first year. The settlers were almost completely without private cash resources, their late arrival precluded any possibility of a crop in 1888, and, as indicated above, their remaining public funds had been entirely used up in the preliminary settlement process. Each family unit, therefore, had to be sustained by its own wages, further public assistance, or a combination of the two. Scarth's demand for an additional £1,400, while including the £720 already agreed to and his company's $1,000 "settlement fee," was explained as being required to pay all costs including one year's maintenance which all Lewis crofters claimed they had been promised. Malcolm McNeill firmly denied that any such promise had been made; Scarth was advised "not to give too ready credence to the statements of the Crofters as to promises made" in Scotland, and the settlers were told that their maintenance was to be covered by the loan each had already received. The report made by the inspecting agent of the Dominion Lands Branch in

September recorded several expressions of dissatisfaction on this point, but the generally prevailing prosperity experienced by the settlers still sustained their optimism. On 15 September, a letter signed by all the Lewis heads of families appeared in *The Winnipeg Morning Call*, categorically denying that they were dissatisfied with their situations in Manitoba as a recent correspondent had suggested.[9]

But the contentment was short lived. The general failure of the potato crop on the rented ground, and the curtailment of threshing work due to an early frost altered the optimistic outlook, particularly of the Killarney crofters. Deciding to press their claim for a year's maintenance, the family heads met at the home of John Nicolson on 4 November 1888. All eighteen family heads signed a petition addressed to the Lord Provost of Glasgow alleging, along with other grievances, that the promise of a year's provisions had been broken and that it would soon be necessary to sell their implements and livestock to buy food. The petition succeeded only in provoking virulent denials from Malcolm McNeill that provisions had been promised, and resulted in the Scottish Office demanding of McNeill a written guarantee that future emigrants would receive no cash advance to pay Scottish debts. In Winnipeg, Scarth decided to send his secretary in the company of Richard Waugh, the editor of the *Nor' West Farmer*, to Killarney to investigate grievances. Both reported back to Scarth by 14 November, and while neither recorded any sympathy for the settlers' situation, they noted the bitter and unanimous complaint amongst the Lewis crofters that the promise of provision had been broken. Waugh stated that "about one-half of the crofters" would require assistance until a crop could be harvested. Scarth notified the Commissioner for Dominion Lands in Winnipeg, Henry Hall Smith, who immediately forwarded Waugh's report to Ottawa. On 26 November, the Canadian Minister of the Interior, Edgar Dewdney, cabled Tupper in London:

> Some crofters likely to suffer this winter for food. Imperial Government should forthwith provide supplies. Deeds from North West Land Company not given Crofters[,] therefore can give no lien.[10]

This "disquieting telegram" arrived precisely at the moment when parliamentary funding for the settlement scheme was most in doubt and the Under-Secretary for Scotland admitted that "the whole question of colonization to the Manitoba districts" could be affected. To further complicate matters, one of the Harris men died on 21 November, and the administrative ICB in Britain had not yet been appointed. The Scottish Office felt it was in no position to formally ask the Treasury for more money and another flurry of letters and telegrams followed from CNWL officials in Edinburgh and Winnipeg. The Canadian government, as indicated in Dewdney's telegram, claimed it was legally unable to act because, without title to the land, the settlers could give no security for provisions, and because, as the homestead sites were still legally CNWL holdings, they were not subject to federal jurisdiction.

The matter was handled "unofficially" on both sides of the Atlantic. At the request of W.H. Smith,[11] who personally undertook responsibility for the expenditure, Tupper cabled from London that the necessary assistance should be provided. Though Smith's private guarantee was never made public, this very unusual action by the Conservative House Leader in Britain was behind the belief — long held by Killarney area merchants — that all expenses concerning the crofters would be guaranteed by government. Henry Hall Smith, representing the Canadian government, visited Killarney and was able to secure the assurances of local shopkeepers that the crofters would receive all necessary credit during the winter. The visit was pivotal. Both the local shopkeepers and the CNWL considered that the result of Smith's discussions in Killarney was that the British and Canadian governments were committed to the success of the colonization scheme. The company and the shopkeepers extended credit particularly to the Killarney group which, significantly, made no further protest during the winter about broken promises. Whether the obligations of repayment were understood by the crofters is uncertain, but clearly they concurred with the shopkeepers in the opinion that this was not to be a source of concern.

That the Argyle crofters at no time acted in concert with the Killarney crofters during this crisis is curious and deserves comment. With the exception of Roderick Mackay who possessed private resources of £45, the Harris emigrants had arrived in an even more destitute condition than those from Lewis. But their group of twelve families contained seventeen unmarried females of working age, whereas the Lewis group contained only seven among eighteen families. In 1889 three of the Argyle seventeen were reported to be married and nine were reported to be working for wages; in 1889 at Killarney, only four of the seven unmarried females were working for wages. Fragmentary evidence strongly suggests that this pattern was established very soon after the June 1888 arrival. The Argyle settlers, therefore, could depend on a significant income from female family members, while most Killarney crofters could not. When the early frost curtailed male employment on the threshing gangs, the Killarney settlers felt the wage reduction much more severely than their neighbours to the north in Argyle township. Richard Waugh also noted that, even in early

November, most young men from the Argyle settlement were still out earning wages on the threshing gangs despite the early frost. Significantly, when interviewed by the ICB's new agent the following April, the Harris families almost invariably referred to the "kindness" of neighbours and Pelican Lake's bountiful supply of fish; the Lewis families, closer to Killarney, referred only to the "kindness" of the village merchant, T.J. Lawlor.[12] On 10 December 1888 a letter from Kenneth MacMillan of the Argyle settlement appeared in the *Glasgow Herald*. It commented very favourably on the settlement scheme and stood in sharp contrast to the recently publicized petition from the Killarney settlers. Whether solicited or spontaneous, the letter indicated that the two closely related settlements were perceiving "Manitoba" very differently.

The promise to supply the crofters appears to have applied to provisions only. The Killarney merchant, T.J. Lawlor, found it necessary to contact Henry Hall Smith in Winnipeg in the early spring to have arrangements made to supply seed grain. Years later, Lawlor chastized the Scottish Office:

> Fancy a people taken away from fishing scenes and dumped upon the prairie — and no provision made for seed. Gaelic may be a very nice and expressive dialect but you cannot raise wheat from it, and these people had nothing else.[13]

Smith reluctantly sought and gained approval for a further advance. Seed grain and seed potatoes were distributed by the ICB's newly appointed Gaelic-speaking agent in early April. The agent noted much anxiety at that time caused by the news that the next group of crofters was not to be located near Pelican Lake. Many viewed this development as another broken promise. The agent allowed himself to comment in his report (unwisely, as it turned out) that to fail to live up to promises was "breaking faith with the people." Symbolic of the careless attitude of the Canadian government towards the crofter scheme, the agent's report was "discovered" in a basket of arrears in Ottawa fourteen months after it was submitted.

Later in the spring than their neighbours, the crofters planted seed grain in Canadian soil for the first time. The cost of the winter's provisions and the spring advance for seed grain totalled nearly £400. This sum, unlike the £720 granted at Scarth's requests, was distributed fairly equally amongst the thirty families. By April 1889, instead of the £3,600 originally contemplated, £4,720, or an average of over £157 per family head, had been advanced to the Pelican Lake settlers.

ARRIVAL IN ASSINIBOIA

Attention in the spring of 1889 shifted to the forty-nine families about to leave Scotland on 3 April. The CNWL did not wish to repeat its extended disputes with the Scottish Office. Its refusal to have any further involvement in the settlement scheme, and the Department of the Interior's recommendation that land selections be made by "a duly-accredited agent," had resulted in the appointment of a Gaelic-speaking Calgary resident, Grant MacKay, as the Canadian agent of the ICB. Beginning his duties on 18 March, MacKay was instructed to maintain a strict economy and to work closely with Henry Hall Smith. As Dominion Lands Commissioner at Winnipeg, Smith had been involved in the protracted correspondence over the winter required to settle questions that had arisen over the liens taken from the Pelican Lake crofters and the exchange of lands with the CNWL. Neither question had been settled by the time the *Scandinavian* left Glasgow, but Smith was urging that "the trouble and confusion" of the previous year not be repeated. In February, seventy-six quarter sections had been nominally reserved at Wolseley. The delay in parliamentary approval of further emigration in the United Kingdom, however, meant that no inspections or practical preparations for settlement took place before MacKay's appointment. When MacKay met Smith in Winnipeg in early April for the first time to make arrangements for land selection, the forty-nine families were already en route.

Complications arose immediately. The ICB had been embarrassed by charges that the 1888 settlers, by locating on company-owned lands, had been deprived of their right, under the "pre-emption" provisions of the *Dominion Lands Act*, to acquire a second quarter section after three years' residence. A substantial and extended debate on this point occurred in the Montreal press in September and October 1888. More importantly, the ICB had been convinced by Scarth that the government advance was better secured on 320 acres than on 160, and therefore instructed MacKay that each family head should receive a half section. Sir Charles Tupper, travelling to Vancouver on other business, told a surprised Smith on 8 April in Winnipeg that the pre-emption provision had been promised to the emigrants. Inspectors' reports from Wolseley confirmed that the government lands were inadequate to satisfy this requirement. In a frantic series of cables, Smith attempted to persuade the Department of the Interior to exchange certain sections with the CPR and to make available for settlement the sections reserved for schools. On 10 April, the request for school sections was firmly denied. On the morning of 14 April, the Department of the Interior in Ottawa received telegrams from Smith stating that only three CPR sections were suitable and that settlement at

Wolseley was impossible without the school sections. The Department of the Interior received another telegram from Halifax stating that the crofter party was leaving immediately for Wolseley.[14]

For the second time, a land company stepped forward. Ironically, the land company that came to the rescue was the Canadian affiliate of the same land company with which negotiations had broken down a year earlier in Scotland. The Manitoba and North Western Railway Company (MNWR) brought to Smith's attention two townships in an area further west than the previously rejected Churchbridge. The company promised the assistance of its agents in settling the crofters and persuaded Smith to visit the lands in question. At 9:23 a.m. on 15 April, Smith again advised Dewdney that settlement at Wolseley was impossible; at 9:25 a.m., from the same office, the MNWR renewed its offer. The Department of the Interior had no choice. Less than twenty-four hours from Winnipeg, the new immigrants were told that their destination was no longer Wolseley, but rather Saltcoats, at the terminus of the Manitoba and North Western Railway, in Assiniboia. Surprisingly, no one officially advised British authorities of the change of location. The Scottish Office was informed on 16 May by the smug Glasgow agent of the Commercial Colonisation Company; Colmer, to his considerable embarrassment and annoyance, first learned of the change from newspaper reports in mid-May.

Sir Charles Tupper inspected the land upon his return from the West Coast and sang its praises when he personally welcomed the crofter train at Winnipeg. The emigrants were in the care of George Betts Borradaile, who had been appointed, at Tupper's suggestion, to meet the *Scandinavian* at Halifax and to supervise the party en route. At Winnipeg, Grant MacKay and A.F. Eden, land commissioner of the MNWR, joined the train which then departed for Saltcoats. During the nighttime journey, the crofter party could see little of the monotonous prairie landscape through which the train was passing. At Churchbridge, MacKay and Borradaile woke the party to prepare for the arrival at Saltcoats very early in the morning of Sunday, 20 April 1889. The residents of Saltcoats village welcomed the new arrivals by providing a hot breakfast; a Gaelic sermon was delivered by a Presbyterian minister, who was present at the request of Canadian government officials at Winnipeg. Two days later, one of the new arrivals married her fiancé — one of the 1888 emigrants to Pelican Lake — in a ceremony conducted in the Saltcoats railway station. The celebration ended with the giving of gifts and a speech of appreciation to the townsfolk by Grant MacKay. In a fine example of civic boosterism, the Saltcoats correspondent of the *Manitoba Free Press* wrote:

> Three cheers were given for the young couple, for the Crofters,
> the musicians and for the Queen, bringing to a happy close a
> red letter day in the history of the rising city of Saltcoats.[15]

The outlook of the new settlers, however, was far from the spirit of
optimism conveyed by the newspaper reporter. Having endured the political debate in Scotland, having had their destination changed twice in
two months, and having just completed a journey that many later
recalled as particularly arduous, the crofter party arrived at Saltcoats sick
and dispirited. The medical doctor, who at the end of April located at
Saltcoats at A.F. Eden's particular request, wrote that a "combination of
seasickness, trainsickness and homesickness bedeviled the immigrants."[16] One adult and two children died shortly after arrival and the
treatment of others was hindered by their complete inability to pay for
doctor's fees and prescribed medicine. The often irrational and inconsistent behaviour of many of the settlers subsequent to their arrival is best
viewed as an attempt to reestablish control of their own destinies, to convince themselves that leaving the Islands had indeed been their best
choice. At almost every turn, the evidence was contrary.

A.F. Eden ordered the company's Saltcoats agent, Thomas MacNutt,[17]
to suspend all other business in order to assist with the settlement of the
crofters. MacNutt, Eden, MacKay and Borradaile all were involved in the
settlement process, though surviving records give little indication of the
roles played by Borradaile and MacKay. The MNWR officials appear to
have initially decided upon the homestead locations with little regard for
the settlers' preferences. Each family head was conveyed to the site chosen for him approximately ten miles north of Saltcoats; forty-six initially
refused to accept the selections. MacNutt later stated that the parish
groups wanted to settle together, and the eventual settlement pattern did
reflect Scottish parish origins. Fourteen families insisted on locations of a
more purely prairie character than those the company was offering. That
group settled in an adjacent township on land the company had not intended to offer. As much as a month was taken up by the process of site
selection. Eden stated that in all his not inconsiderable experience, he had
"never found a more difficult lot of men to satisfy."[18]

Some of the men, under the impression that houses were to be built *for*
them and not *by* them, refused to unload and haul their own lumber unless paid to do so. To avoid further delay they were paid ten cents an
hour. The amounts were later charged against their advances. When the
process was finally complete, only twenty-four families had entered for
pre-emptions. Twelve families ultimately accepted the sites originally
chosen for them; twenty-four made selections on lands not originally

offered; eleven chose sites rejected by others. The twelve who accepted their original sites apparently were located on the best soil in the area, but many of the original sites rejected were broken up by large sloughs.[19] Two families left the area before making selections to join relatives at Moosomin and Killarney. Twenty-four families were located on government lands; twenty-three on lands belonging to the MNWR. Two distinct colonies had been formed. Fourteen families were clustered in Township 24, Ranges 2 and 3, northwest of Leech Lake, and became known as the King Colony; thirty-three families located in Township 25, Ranges 1, 2, and 3, the area originally offered by the company, and became known as the Lothian Colony.

The inadequacy of available funds was soon revealed even more clearly at Saltcoats than it had been at Pelican Lake. Despite Scottish Office attempts to reduce family size and to select families with private means, despite fare reductions from the Allan Line and the CPR, despite the example of the Pelican Lake experience, the Saltcoats settlers were seriously underfunded. This was severely complicated by the instruction to MacKay not to advance funds to any individual family member other than the family head. Whether the ICB was concerned about the legality of such advances or whether the decision was linked to the promise of pre-emption rights cannot be stated with certainty. However, the practical result was to restrict funds to designated family heads and to prohibit any increase in those funds as had occurred at Pelican Lake. Though the average amount available to each family head for expenditure in Canada was nearly £85, MacKay was informed from London that seventeen would have less than £80, that he should initially restrict his expenditure to £70 per family, and that out of that sum he was to have "particular regard to the first winter's requirements." Exclusive of provisions, $300 was determined as the maximum sum available per family for settlement purposes.[20] That is to say, the maximum available was precisely half the sum acknowledged by the *Dominion Lands Act* to be necessary for settlement and farm-establishment purposes.

MacKay and the MNWR officials were obliged to economize wherever possible. Later complaints from the crofters that the food and livestock provided them were inferior were always vigorously denied by the ICB. However, smaller houses than those originally contemplated were erected. These were constructed with third-grade lumber, and were intended to last only a few years. MacKay attempted to follow his instructions closely and, much to the irritation of the supplier, Buchanan and Company of Saltcoats, issued hundreds of itemized vouchers rather than approve a general provision of a few weeks' supply. A system of sharing oxen, ploughs, and harnesses was attempted, with each family head being charged only half the cost of each. Even before the settlers' arrival, it had been anticipated that this system would prove unworkable. Sir Charles Tupper, while in Winnipeg, secured the agreement of the MNWR that it would provide the additional funds to allow each family head a yoke of oxen and a wagon. Tupper agreed to attempt to secure further Imperial funds, up to £60 per family, but if he was unsuccessful, the company was to repossess the oxen and wagons.

The chaotic settlement process at Saltcoats was considered by Tupper to have gone "less smoothly" than it should have done. Perhaps not unexpectedly, considering the statement about "breaking faith" contained in his report from Pelican Lake in April, the ICB's agent, Grant MacKay, was deemed to be lacking in energy and good judgement and was dismissed by the ICB on 18 June. By mid-June, Henry Hall Smith advised Ottawa that MacKay had given advances in excess of available funds and that unless the additional money Tupper sought arrived immediately, the colony's failure was inevitable. When it was realized that MacKay had not taken liens on chattels before his dismissal, Borradaile's temporary appointment was extended to the end of July by a grumbling Department of the Interior which inadvertently found itself responsible for his $75 monthly salary.

With MacKay's dismissal, the Winnipeg Dominion Lands office once again found itself bearing the primary responsibility for the entire scheme. During the first few days of July, Henry Hall Smith received a letter from A.F. Eden alleging that the Saltcoats settlers were grossly underfunded, and a letter from the doctor at Saltcoats stating that he and the druggist had "indulged in all the philanthropy and charity" they could afford. At the same time, he received notification that several Killarney families claimed destitution was upon them, and he read in the *Manitoba Free Press* a petition from the Saltcoats crofters stating that his department would be breaking faith with the settlers if it allowed Borradaile's temporary appointment to expire.[21] By early July, it became apparent that the 1889 crops would be light due to drought conditions in Manitoba and Assiniboia. In late June, just as the Colonisation Committee in London called its first witness on crofter emigration, Borradaile placed a public notice at the Buchanan store in Saltcoats stating that all credits to crofters were suspended.

Smith was thoroughly alarmed. He warned the Minister of the Interior that trouble was imminent and suggested that if the person superintending the settlements was in the employ of the Department of the Interior, the Department would be held responsible. Though he suspected that Borradaile was responsible for the *Free Press* petition, Smith urged that the ICB should be pressed to appoint him as its agent, as he was the only one sufficiently familiar with the new settlement's affairs. The Department agreed. A.M. Burgess, the Deputy Minister of the Department of the Interior, wrote to Dewdney:

> The position we occupy at the present time is an embarrassing one in every respect. We are made to shoulder the mistakes of the Imperial Government, who apparently turn a deaf ear to our representations; ... I think they ought to bear the whole responsibility themselves, and the expense as well. At all events, neither the responsibility nor the expense properly belongs to this Department.[22]

Dewdney cabled Tupper on 9 July:

> Smith represents necessary immediately appoint Borradaile agent Colonization Board finish up Crofters' business, otherwise grave complications certain.[23]

On 10 July, Dewdney was informed that the British Treasury had agreed to the appointment of Borradaile at $1,000 per year, plus the expense of a horse. No one stopped to consider that the new Canadian agent spoke no Gaelic. Once again, the ICB had taken up its only available option.

On 15 August 1889, the Scottish Office finally received the Treasury's reluctant agreement that £1,500, the unexpended portion of the original £10,000 voted in April 1888, would be included in a Supplementary Estimate. Pointedly stating the "awkward matter" of varying a parliamentary Minute, the Treasury argued that only the peculiar nature of the emigration experiment permitted an expense that would otherwise have been unjustifiable. The request for £385 for administrative expenses was also allowed.[24] Tupper claimed that he had personally lobbied every important government figure in order to secure these amounts. Colmer advised Borradaile on 2 August — before official confirmation from the Treasury — that his appointment was confirmed and that £1,800 would be sent in a few days. The MNWR was to receive $4,085 for the oxen and ploughs it had provided, and T.J. Lawlor at Killarney was to receive $2,000 for the seed grain and the provisions personally guaranteed by W.H. Smith. The remaining $3,000 was intended to pay overdrawn merchants' accounts at Saltcoats and to provide for maintenance during the coming winter at Saltcoats.

With questions of liens and land transfers at Killarney still unresolved and with the Saltcoats settlement so problematic, Tupper decided to send Colmer to visit Ottawa, Winnipeg, and the settlements in the autumn of 1889. At Ottawa, Colmer found the Department of the Interior adamant that it bore no responsibility for Lothian's scheme, doubtful that debt-ridden settlements had any chance of success, and prone to comparing the crofters with "helpless" Northwest Indians. The Department was, however, willing to involve itself in an advisory capacity and agreed that its Land Commissioner at Winnipeg should continue to assist Borradaile and would continue to act as a signing officer for the ICB. In Winnipeg, Colmer met with representatives of the land companies and suggested the establishment of an honourary subcommittee to assist the ICB in administration of the crofter settlements. The land company officials all expressed a willingness to further the immigration interests of the Northwest in this manner. Since negotiations between the CNWL and the Canadian government over the land transfers at Pelican Lake were still proceeding, Colmer was unable to complete arrangements to transfer the liens to the ICB. In fact, he found that the CNWL liens themselves were far from being complete and, at his insistence, company officials remained at Killarney until all but three were completed by 2 November.

At Pelican Lake, Colmer visited all the homesteads of heads of families. He reported that their houses were warm and comfortable, all being double-boarded, packed with clay or soil, and measuring fourteen feet by sixteen feet. Each family head had approximately forty acres ready for seeding, although eighteen homesteads were having problems securing a water supply. Due to drought conditions, crops had not been marketable, but were thought to be sufficient for the settlers' own needs in the coming winter. Twenty-six adults (including one family head) from the Lewis portion of the settlement were working for wages, as were twenty-two adults from the Harris portion. Apart from a concern about seed grain for the coming year (expressed by two family heads without adult help), Colmer told the ICB that he heard of no complaints of a significant nature from any of the settlers and that, with "ordinary good fortune," the success of the settlement was assured.

Of the settlement near Saltcoats, Colmer could not express the same degree of optimism. The lengthy delays in site selection and house construction, the resultant delay in ploughing and planting, and the drought conditions had combined to leave the settlers with no crop whatsoever. Winter provisions were to be provided by Borradaile from the ICB's $3,000 remaining credit. Clothing supplies were found to be inadequate for the approaching winter, and Colmer managed to arrange a charitable collection of clothing in Winnipeg. The drought had created difficulties in securing winter hay supplies and in sinking wells. In October, fewer than a dozen houses were ready for winter and one family head was still living in a tent. A sum of $300 for public works was secured by Tupper

from the Lieutenant-Governor of the North-West Territories specifically
to provide local employment for the crofters on railway bed preparation
on the extension to Yorkton. Otherwise, local employment was scarce. At
least nine younger men had left for employment at Portage la Prairie by
12 May, and were later joined by others. Forty-nine adults were working
for wages in locations ranging from the Rocky Mountains to Rat Portage.
Significantly, thirty had sent no money home by the date of Colmer's
visit. Only ten family heads had broken more than ten acres and very
little of this was backset. Numerous complaints were made to Colmer.
Demonstrating a chilling lack of understanding of what is significant to
both experienced and novice farmers, Colmer reported that these complaints "were more or less of an unimportant nature, relating to the
quality of the provisions, to the cattle supplied to them, to the prices
charged, and other similar matters."[25] As Colmer gave Borradaile instructions on how to deal with these "minor" complaints, neither man could
have realized that for the next fifteen years the primary responsibility for
managing the crofter settlements at Pelican Lake and Saltcoats was to fall
upon their own shoulders.

CHAPTER FOUR

Settlements and Administration to 1893

As INDICATED in the previous chapter, welcoming committees and celebrations awaited the crofter immigrants in the Canadian West. At Pelican Lake, the settlers received community assistance in the form of leased potato land and voluntary carpentry work. At Saltcoats, the much smaller population was unable to provide similar material assistance to the newcomers. But the disappointment expressed by Wolseley residents at the last-minute change of location indicates that the arrival of such a large group of settlers would have been favourably regarded by any settler community in the Northwest during this period of disappointingly low immigration. There is no reason to believe that the residents of Saltcoats or Killarney would have dissented from the good will expressed by the "Welcome to the Crofters" editorial that appeared in the *Manitoba Free Press* on 4 June 1888.

Though evidence is fragmentary, enough exists to suggest that relations between the host communities and the crofters became strained very soon after the settlers arrived. Coming from the Western Isles, the crofters had left a political environment that had for several years encouraged the articulation of protest and grievance. Believing that the contract that placed them on the Canadian Prairies entailed obligations on the part of the British government, and believing that some of those obligations were being avoided, the settlers did not hesitate to voice their concerns to anyone who would listen. Even when the grievances were expressed in the form of private letters or petitions to Scottish dignitaries (such as the petition of November 1888 to the Lord Provost of Glasgow), the local population at Saltcoats and Killarney became aware of the problems either because local inquiries were made by government officials or because the crofters themselves publicized their activities. This chapter examines the early relationships the crofters developed with their administrators and their local communities.

PELICAN LAKE: THE FIRST FIVE YEARS

From the moment they left the Islands, the Pelican Lake settlers became a "new card" in the debate over land reform in the Highlands, and improvements in communications technology meant that they could not be isolated from that debate. In early September 1888, statements by

John McIver, an agricultural labourer who had travelled independently with the Lewis emigrants aboard the *Corean,* were published in both Canada and Britain. McIver spoke of oppressive heat, exploitation of female labour, and deaths in the settlements. He referred to Manitoba as a "perfect hell" and said that the emigrants wanted to warn friends and relatives not to join them at Pelican Lake. All of this, of course, was perfectly in keeping with the anti-emigration campaign of the Land League back in Scotland. Officials in the Scottish Office speculated, probably quite correctly, that McIver was an agent of the Land League, in Manitoba specifically to discredit the colonization scheme.

The new settlers, however, were still in their honeymoon stage at Pelican Lake, and their Canadian neighbours were concerned with other issues — namely, the settlement and development of the Canadian West. For the first time, therefore, the Lewis crofters gathered for a political purpose, and issued a statement that was signed by all eighteen family heads and published in the Winnipeg press:

> We, the undersigned, being heads of the families of crofters who came to Pelican Lake from the Lews in Scotland this year, having read the above cable sent from London on the 6th of September and published in the *Winnipeg Morning Call* beg to give the statements therein our most emphatic contradiction. We are quite satisfied with the country. We never entreated McIver to warn our friends not to come out, but on the contrary in their own interests think they ought to come. The heat and water are not killing us. The only death that has taken place among us was immediately on our arrival, and was that of a young child. As many of our daughters as desire it can get work among neighboring farmers or in villages and towns throughout the country at respectable places and at good wages. All the young men who have desired work have also been able to get it among farmers or on the Canadian Pacific Railway at good wages.[1]

The Canadians were well pleased at this expression of satisfaction. So, too, was the Scottish Office. The letter, in English and Gaelic, was printed and distributed by Malcolm McNeill in Lewis to encourage the emigration of 1889.

Relations with neighbours at Pelican Lake took a turn for the worse as the issue of the first winter's maintenance emerged. The keeper of a boarding house in Killarney visited the Lewis crofters to insist they should not send negative reports back to Scotland. The farmer who had rented the potato ground in June expressed the opinion in November that the crofters had "lowered the character of the settlement." Visiting

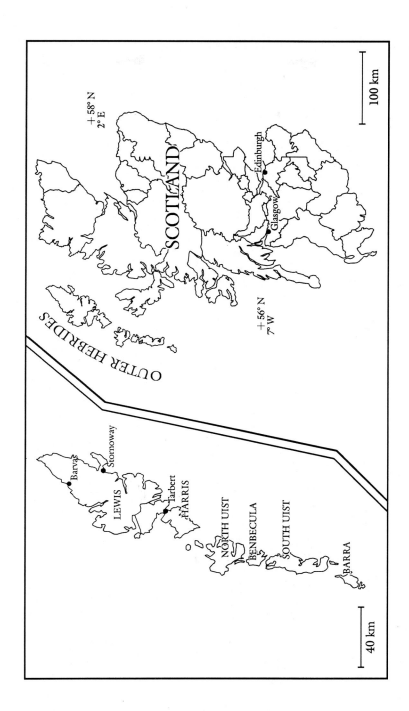

Late nineteenth-century Scotland showing the Outer Hebrides (Western Isles)

THE SCOTCH CROFTERS IN MANITOBA.

The following extract from Canadian newspapers refers to the statements of John M'Iver which have recently been published.

The "Call" has made inquiries respecting this John M'Iver, and in an interview with Mr. Scarth, M.P., the facts regarding his case were learned. It appears from these that he came out here with a colony of crofters under the arrangement made with the Imperial Government, but was not himself one of those who had taken advantage of the terms offered. He was, however, assisted to a considerable extent, but his name not appearing among those on the list sent out to Mr. Scarth, he could not, of course, be placed on land on the same terms as the others. It is not probable that this troubled him to any great extent, as it appears that he preferred city to country life, and his habits here do not seem to have been of the kind to ensure success. The particulars given by Mr. Scarth of M'Iver's stay in Manitoba will not lead any one to place much reliance on the latter's description of the experiences of actual settlers. His statement that immigrants settled here had entreated him to warn their friends not to come out receives most effectual contradiction in a letter to the "Glasgow Herald" by its special correspondent whom it had sent out here particularly to visit the crofter settlements. That correspondent said he had interviewed several of the settlers and that they all declare themselves highly delighted with the change they have made, and confident of success.

M'Iver's assertion in regard to the daughters of immigrants is so absurdly untrue that it would be laughable were it not possible that the report may produce a serious check to the further immigration of females to this country. There are very few households in Winnipeg, or in other towns in Manitoba and the North-West, where great difficulty has not been experienced in securing domestics, and all girls who have heretofore come out to this country and who have desired to obtain employment have quickly secured good situations and at very lucrative figures. In fact, the wages paid here to servants is considerably higher than is paid in many of the eastern towns of Canada or the United States. A girl who receives ten, twelve, or fifteen dollars a month, in a comfortable household, has nothing to complain of, and when M'Iver draws his dark picture of the immigrant girl's life here he is deliberately falsifying the situation. His declaration that Manitoba was a "perfect hell" caps the climax of his exaggerated stories, and gives one a pretty fair idea of the kind of man he is.

WHAT THE CROFTERS THEMSELVES SAY.

The crofters themselves have also had something to say in reply to Mr. M'Iver's misrepresentations. Their statement, as published in the Winnipeg papers, is as follows :—

We, the undersigned, being heads of the families of crofters who came to Pelican Lake from the Lews in Scotland this year, having read the above cable sent from London on the 6th of September and published in the "Winnipeg Morning Call," beg to give the statements therein our most emphatic contradiction. We are quite satisfied with the country. We never entreated M'Iver to warn our friends not to come out, but on the contrary in their own interests think they ought to come. The heat and water are not killing us. The only death that has taken place among us was immediately on our arrival, and was that of a young child. As many of our daughters as desire it can get work among neighbouring farmers or in villages and towns throughout the country at respectable places and at good wages. All the young men who have desired work have also been able to get it among farmers or on the Canadian Pacific Railway at good wages.

(Signed) John McLeod, Wm. McLeod, Jno. McKenzie, Sen., Jno. Graham, Angus McLeod, Jno. Morrison, Jno. McKenzie, Jun., Wm. McDonald, John Nicholson, Kenneth MacAulay, Angus McDonald, Murdo Graham, John McKay, Norman McKenzie, Allan McLeod, Jno. Campbell, Norman Graham, Donald McDonald.

Killarney, Manitoba, September 15th, 1888.

Our girls are getting from 10 to 12 dollars a month, and the men are getting from 20 to 30 dollars a month, and as for the women, they are gaining in flesh in the place of dying. We can get plenty of good water by digging wells.

Yours truly,
JOHN McLEOD, Fairhall P.O.

o 56608.   800.—12/88. Wt. 16531. E. & S.

Leaflet distributed in the Highlands in 1888 to counter negative reports about conditions at Pelican Lake.

NA CROITEARAN ALBANNACH ANN AM MANITOBA.

So sios bideagan a litrichean-naigheachd Chanada mu dheibhinn aithris Iain Mhic Iomhair :—

An deigh ransachadh ma Iain Mac Iomhair, agus Maighstir Scarth, M.P., fhaicinn, 's e so am fios a fhuair an " Call" ma 'n chuis. A reir coltais, thainig Iain a mach le cuideachda chroitearan, fo chordadh a chaidh dheanamh ris an Riaghladh Iompaireil, ach cha robh esa na fhear de 'n t-sluagh a dh' iarr feum a dheanamh a tairgsean a chumhnaint. A dh' aindeoin sin, cha deach fhagail gun chomhnadh cuimseach, ach leis nach robh ainm, am measg chaich, air a chlar-ainmean a chaidh chuir a dh' ionnsuidh Maighstir Scarth, bha e eu-comasach a chuir air fearann air an aon bhonn ris na daoin' eile. Theagamh nach do chuir sin moran smuairein air, oir tha e coltach gu 'm bu docha leis beatha baile na beatha duthcha, agus nach robh a ghnathachadh an so de 'n t-seorsa a ni soirbheachadh cinnteach. Cha d' thoir an cunntas sonruichte, a thug Maighstir Scarth ma fhuireach Iain Mhic Iomhair ann am Manitoba, neach sam bith gu creideas mor a chuir anns na thubhairt e ma chor 's ma fhaireachduinn an t-sluaigh a shuidhich air an fhearann. Chaidh a sgeul, gu'n do ghuidh iadsan a thainig a mach iar rabhadh a thoirt do 'n cairdean gun an leanachd, aicheadh gu laidir ann an litir do 'n "Ghlasgow Herald," o 'n duine a chuir am paipeir sin do 'n duthaich so a choimhead, gu sonruichte, air gach aiteachas a fhuair na croitearan. Thuirt an duine sin gu'n robh comhradh aige ri iomadh fear-suidhichte, agus gu 'n d'innis iad uile dha gu'n robh iad ro-thoilichte le 'n imirich, agus cinnteach air soirbheachadh.

Tha aithris Mhic Iomhair, a thaobh nigheanan nan daoine a thainig a nall, neo-fhirinneach air sheol cho mhichiallach agus gu 'm b'ann a b'aobhar ghaire i, air bhith gu 'm faodadh a leithid de sgeul boirionnaich a bhacadh o thighinn do 'n duthaich so. 'S gann fardach an Winnipeg, am bailtean eile Mhanitoba, 's anns an Tuath-Iar, aig nach 'eil fhios cho duilich 's a tha e seirbheisich-thaighe fhaotainn ; agus gus a so, fhuair na nigheanan uile, a thainig a mach 's a dh'iarr sin, deagh aiteachan, gle ealamh, 's le duais arda. A dh' innseadh na firinn 's ann a tha seirbheisich, an so, a faotainn duais durc na 's airde na gheibh iad ann am bailtean shios Chanada, 's anns na Staidean. Cha 'n eil aobhar gearain aig nighean a tha coisneadh, ann an taigh somulta, deich, dusan, na coig-deug dollar 's a mhios ; agus ann an tarruinn dealbh dubh de bheatha na caileige a thainig a mach, 's ann a tha Mac Iomhair coltach ri bhith cuir roimhe dol an aghaidh na firinn. Ach chuir e ceann paip uile air a sgeulachd leis na facail gur "nubh ifrinn" Manitoba ; agus o sin faodar a thuigsinn de'n seorsa duine a th'ann.

FREAGAIRT NAN CROITEARAN FHEIN.

Cha d' fhan na croitearan iad fhein na 'n tosd mu thimchioll mi-aithris Mhic Iomhair. So an fhreagairt a thug iad ann an litrichean-naigheachd Winnipeg :—

Air dhuinne, a tha fodh-sgriobhte, cinn-theaghlaichean chroitearan a thainig, am bliadhna, gu Loch a Phelicain o Leoghas, ann an Albainn, an sgeul-taoid a Lunnuinn, air an t-seathamh latha de mhios mheadhonnach an fhoghair, a leughadh, anns an "Winnipeg Morning Call," tha sinn ag iarraidh na h-agairtean a fhuair sinn an sin aicheadh ro-bhuileach. Cha do ghuidh sinn riamh air Mac Iomhair rabhadh a thoirt do 'r cairdean gun tighinn a mach, ach an aite sin is e ar baral gur coir dhoibh tighinn a mach airson am math fhein. Cha 'n eil teas agus uisge ga 'r marbhadh. Cha do bhasaich neach 'n ar measg ach aon leanamh og, a chaochail cho luath 's a thainig sinn gu 'r ceann-uidhe. 'S urrainn uibhir de ar nigheanan 's a tha 'g iarraidh sin, deagh aiteachan agus deagh dhuais fhaotainn feadh thuathanach na coimhearsnachd, na anns na bailtean beaga agus mora feadh na duthcha. 'S urrainn na gillean oga uile, a tha deigheil air a sin, obair le duais mhath fhaotainn feadh nan tuathanach, na air Rathad-iaruinn Chanada Pacific.

(Fodh-sgriobhte le)—Iain Mac Leoid, Uilleam Mac Leoid, Seann Iain Mac Coinnich, Iain Graham, Aonghas Mac Leoid, Iain Morrison, Iain Og Mac Coinnich, Uilleam Mac Dhomhnuill, Iain Nicholson, Coinneach Mac Aulay, Aonghas Mac Dhomhnuill, Murchadh Graham, Iain Mac Aoidh, Tormod Mac Coinnich, Ailean Mac Leoid, Iain Caimbeul, Tormod Graham, Domhnull Mac Dhomhnuill.

Killarney, Manitoba, September 15, *1888.*

Tha ar nigheanan a coisneadh eadar deich agus dusan dollar 's a mhios, tha na daoine a deanamh eadar fichead agus deich thar fhichead dollar 's a mhios, agus an aite do na mnathan a bhith basachadh 's ann a tha iad a fas reamhar. 'S urrainn duinn pailteas uisge fhaotainn le tobraichean a chladhachadh.

Gu dilens dhuibhse,

IAIN MAC LEOID, Fairhall P.O.

Stornoway Castle, Lewis. Courtesy Lois Klaassen.

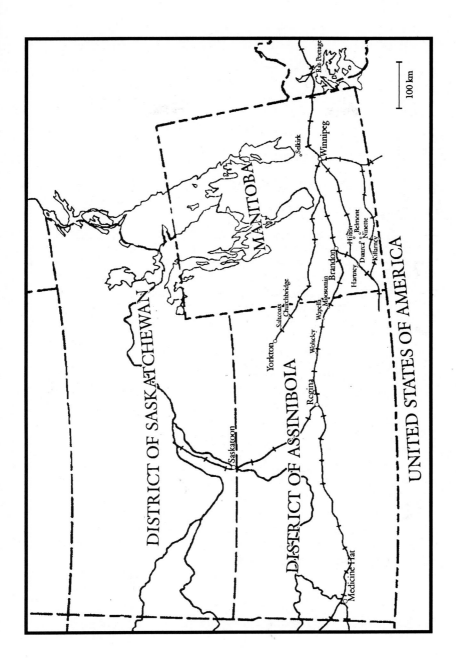

Manitoba and Assiniboia, c. 1890.

V. 🦁 R.

The SECRETARY FOR SCOTLAND is enabled to offer EMIGRATION to CANADA, during the Spring of 1889, to a few selected families on the following terms:—

1. £120 will be advanced for each household, out of which will be provided travelling and all other expenses, including necessary stock and implements, and the balance will be paid over in the Colony.

2. No repayment will be demanded for four years; but during the succeeding eight years each family will be required to pay £20 17s. 8d. annually, and will then become owners of the Farms.

3. 160 acres of good land will be provided, free of charge, by the Canadian Government for each male head of a family; and the other males above 18 years of age are also entitled, if they desire it, to similar free grants.

4. No family will be selected for Emigration whose expenses, up to the time of arrival at the site of settlement, are likely to exceed £50.

5. A preference must, therefore, be given to those families which can show the possession of private resources.

The Commissioners of the Secretary for Scotland and of the Canadian Government will visit the district, for the purpose of selecting suitable families, on an early date, of which due notice will be given.

LOTHIAN,
H.M.'s Secretary for Scotland.

PRINTED FOR HER MAJESTY'S STATIONERY OFFICE BY ROBSON & SONS, Limited, 20, PANCRAS ROAD, N.W.   (35,647a) 100 8—88

Posters outlining the emigration scheme were quickly torn down by the scheme's opponents in the autumn of 1888.
Courtesy Scottish Record Office (AF 51/89).

Sir Charles Tupper, Canadian High Commissioner in London, 1884-1896.
Courtesy National Archives of Canada (C10109).

(Copy)

3

(A.)

*FORM OF APPLICATION FOR ASSISTANCE
TO EMIGRATE

From the Property of *Lady Weatherson* {State here Name of Proprietor.

(It is requested that if Applicants cannot write distinctly, they will procure assistance in filling up their applications.)

I, *Finlay MacLean* , residing at *North Skabost* , in the parish of *Lochs* , county of *Ross* , hereby request assistance to emigrate to Canada, on the terms stated by the Agent of the Secretary for Scotland; and I engage to present myself, if my application be granted, with the under-noted members of my household, for embarkation on any date and at any port which may be intimated to me.

The total sum at my command, including the value of my stock (consisting of)
is about £ *nil*

And the following list includes all who reside under my roof.

(Signed) *Finlay McLean* , aged *29*

Trade or calling— *Fisherman and Farm-worker*

List of persons, members of his household, to accompany Applicant.

NAME	Relationship to Applicant	Age	Trade or Calling, if any
*Mary	wife	29	Housewife
*John MacLeod	brother-in-law	21	Farm-worker
*Whole party failed to embark			

(Signed) *Finlay McLean* Applicant.

(Signed) *Malcolm McNeill* Witness.

Residing at *Edinburgh*

Designation *Poorlaw Inspector*

* The Government advance will be the same for each family, but a preference will be given to Applicants who can show, in addition, the largest resources.

R & S (32,934a) 300 5—88

[TURN OVER

The Finlay MacLean family was selected to emigrate in 1888, but failed to embark. Courtesy Scottish Record Office (AF 51/36).

(B.)

SCHEDULE FOR EMIGRATION OFFICER.

(To be handed to the Agent in the Colony, and filed by him for reference.)

Name of Emigrant— *Donald MacDonald*

Age— *28*

Trade or Calling— *Sailor and Fisherman, Farm-worker*

Amount of resources in addition to Government advance— *£5*

Parish and county from which removed— *Stornoway, Rofshire*

List of persons, members of his household, accompanying Emigrant.

NAME	Relationship to Emigrant	Age	Trade or Calling, if any
Jessie	*wife*	*26*	*Housewife*
John	*son*	*4*	*Infant*
Margaret	*daughter*	*1¾*	*Do.*
Samuel Graham	*brother-in-law*	*20*	*Farm-worker*
Mary	*sister*	*21*	*Do. Do.*

The Emigration Officer, having ascertained that the household is complete, will append the date of embarkation and his signature.

(Signed) *Malcolm McNeill*

[Date of Embarkation.] *17th May 1888*

(Signed) *Thomas Graham* Emigration Officer.

R & S (32,936a) 350 5—88

The Donald MacDonald family possessed more private resources than most of the emigrant families. Courtesy Scottish Record Office (AF 51/42).

Malcolm McNeill, Poor Law official and originator
of the Lothian emigration scheme.

James Stewart Tupper, son of Sir Charles Tupper and solicitor for the Imperial Colonisation Board. Courtesy Provincial Archives of Manitoba (W10676).

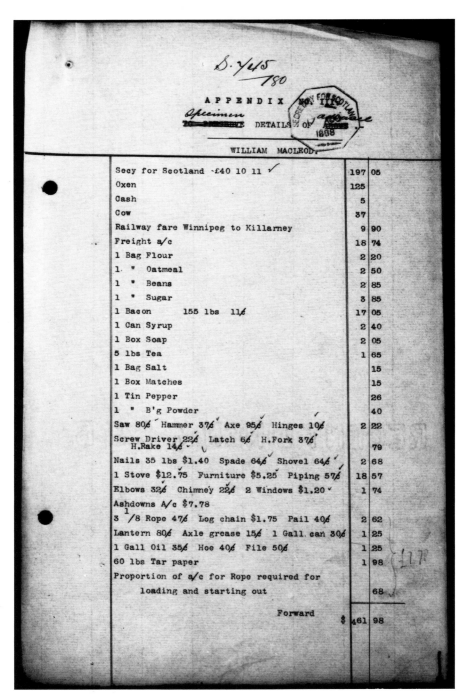

APPENDIX

Specimen

DETAILS OF

WILLIAM MACLEOD.

Secy for Scotland £40 10 11 ✓		197	05
Oxen		125	
Cash		5	
Cow		37	
Railway fare Winnipeg to Killarney		9	90
Freight a/c		18	74
1 Bag Flour		2	20
1 " Oatmeal		2	50
1 " Beans		2	85
1 " Sugar		3	85
1 Bacon 155 lbs 11¢		17	05
1 Can Syrup		2	40
1 Box Soap		2	05
5 lbs Tea		1	65
1 Bag Salt			15
1 Box Matches			15
1 Tin Pepper			26
1 " B'g Powder			40
Saw 80¢ Hammer 37¢ Axe 95¢ Hinges 10¢		2	22
Screw Driver 22¢ Latch 6¢ H.Fork 37¢ H.Rake 14¢			79
Nails 35 lbs $1.40 Spade 64¢ Shovel 64¢		2	68
1 Stove $12.75 Furniture $5.25 Piping 57¢		18	57
Elbows 32¢ Chimney 22¢ 2 Windows $1.20		1	74
Ashdowns A/c $7.78			
3 1/8 Rope 47¢ Log chain $1.75 Pail 40¢		2	62
Lantern 80¢ Axle grease 15¢ 1 Gall. can 30¢		1	25
1 Gall Oil 35¢ Hoe 40¢ File 50¢		1	25
60 lbs Tar paper		1	98
Proportion of a/c for Rope required for			
loading and starting out			68
	Forward	$ 461	98

Transportation and settlement expenses for William MacLeod's party of three
adults, Pelican Lake 1888. Courtesy Scottish Record Office (AF 51/69).

Brought Forward - $	461	98
Ox harness	9	80 ✓
Plough $22.50 Waggon $67.50	90	✓
202ft 2x4=16ft $2.82 32ft 2x4=12 44¢	3	26 ✓
256 " Boards 16ft $3.84 476ft bds		
14ft $6.66	10	50 ✓
400 ft Boards 16ft	6	✓
56 " 2x4 - 14ft		78 ✓
Proportion of Blacksmith's a/c for Clevise's		79 ✓
Supplies on arrival, Lawton's a/c		45 ✓
Harstone Breakfasts in Winnipeg		90 ✓
Gouldie " " Killarney		63 ✓
Proportion of Provisions sent		
to Potato field	1	82 ✓
Proportion of Rent of Potato ground	1	28 ✓
	588	19
Loan	584	00
Excess	4	19
Probable further advances		
Four Homestead Fees	40	
Additional Lumber	12	
Share of Expenses 4 Homesteads	35	
Provisions (cannot give any amount)		

2

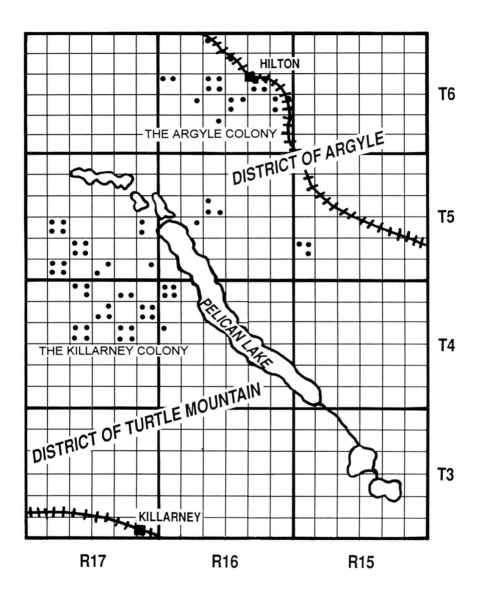

Homestead locations near Pelican Lake, 1888-1906.

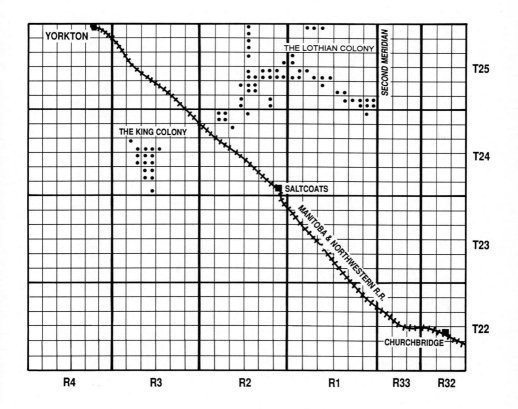

Homestead locations near Saltcoats, 1889-1906.

George Betts Borradaile, Crofter Commissioner 1889-1905.
Courtesy Osmond Borradaile, O.C.

Colin Macleay, Saltcoats area school teacher, c. 1891. Courtesy Marion Hulme.

Lady Aberdeen photographed Murdo Graham and family near Pelican Lake in October 1890. Courtesy of the Earl of Haddo. (Lady Aberdeen identified this settler as Peter Graham, though there was no settler by that name in the Pelican Lake colony. Given the route she was following and assuming the last name to be correct, the settler can only have been Murdo Graham at NW 13.5.17.)

John Campbell and family were photographed by Lady Aberdeen in October 1890 near Pelican Lake. Courtesy of the Earl of Haddo.

John and Christina Graham and daughters. Courtesy Ruth Hosford.

John Nicolson's abandoned homestead near Pelican Lake. Courtesy Lois Klaassen.

The original homestead of Kenneth Macauley near Pelican Lake.

Dunrea, 1900.

The four daughters of Bannatyne and Margaret Mackinnon with their
Canadian children, 1907. Courtesy of Marion Jowsey.

Killarney, Manitoba, 1886.

Killarney, Manitoba, 1902. Courtesy J.A.V. David Museum.

Killarney, Manitoba, 1909.

T.J. Lawlor, Killarney merchant.

the area in November 1888, just as the settlers' concern over their winter provision was increasing, the editor of the *Nor' West Farmer* found that the crofters were full of claims and grievances. He did not hesitate to state the opinion that

> [t]he men who have been sent out are clearly not the class of people wanted out here... [They] are full of their own importance ... and cannot be made to recognise the fact that any one good live Canadian is worth more than two of them.[2]

Others found humour in the fact that the crofters complained of not getting milk from cows suckling calves and of having their chickens freeze to death in the winter.

The strict religious observances of the new settlers also created disharmony. Angus Graham wrote home in July delighting in the fact he had encountered only one Catholic. But the Free Church Sabbatarianism of the crofters contrasted sharply with the more moderate Protestant practices of their "irreligious" neighbours. Men were required to shave on Saturday night and not at all on Sunday. Cows could be milked on Sunday, but the cream could not be separated until Monday. One of the Harris family heads chased fishermen from Pelican Lake on Sundays, threatening to bring charges against them for breaking the sabbath. Employers, too, encountered difficulties with crofter employees. Three young men quit jobs because an employer swore at them; while working at a Killarney hotel, Constance Morrison refused to peel potatoes on Sundays, that task "not falling under the works of necessity and mercy."

The crofters were numerous enough to form distinct groups within the Presbyterian churches. Gaelic services were conducted at Hilton for the Harris crofters and at Bellafield School for the Lewis crofters beginning in August 1888. The permanent appointment of Reverend Gollan in 1889 meant that both colonies could attend regular weekly Gaelic services. Religion, therefore, tended to emphasize the isolation of the crofter groups from the broader community.

The demands of commercial agriculture, on the other hand, would not allow for isolation. Novice farmers are usually regarded by established farmers with a combination of indulgence and condescension. The crofters were no exception. Kenneth Macauley long remembered the mirth that his agricultural naivety caused his employer during that first summer's employment. Generally speaking, the methods of crofting agriculture that were brought from the Scottish Islands were adhered to until proven unsatisfactory. This was especially the case with the older men; commentators noted that the younger men seemed more adaptable and more willing to learn from neighbours. In one respect — which was to cause much heartache in future years — most of the crofters eagerly emulated the example of their neighbours: anticipated crops were mortgaged in order to acquire mowers, rakes, and self-binders.

The agricultural results, from either traditional or modern methods, were not encouraging. The crofters' late arrival in 1888 meant that no crop was possible that year. The drought of 1889 meant that that year's crop was barely enough to maintain the settlers during the winter of 1889-90. Along with their neighbours, the crofters took advantage of Manitoba's *Seed Grain Act* in 1890 to secure seed grain from the municipalities. Crops were more satisfactory in 1890 and 1891, but even the bumper crop of 1892 was severely depreciated by wet weather after harvesting. The Harris portion of the settlement had access to nearby grain elevators at Hilton after 1889, but the Lewis crofters had to haul their grain twelve miles to the elevators at Killarney. The general lack of prosperity is evident in action taken by members of the local business community who, finally realizing that crofter debts would not be paid by the government, began to bring suits against individual crofters in 1891. The debts ranged from $5 to $200 and were mostly for store bills and farming equipment. By early 1894, twenty-five actions had been brought against crofters in the county court of Killarney.[3] It is significant that even John Nicolson, the acknowledged leader and spokesman of the Lewis crofters, was sued for debts twice in 1893. Though "words" do not survive to indicate the views held by local merchants at this time, these "actions" indicate the usual disfavour in which a creditor holds an unsatisfactory debtor.

Despite all the difficulties of adaptation to prairie circumstances, the crofter communities took root. Several marriages amongst the younger crofters took place and, within the first two years of settlement, at least four marriages with non-crofters occurred. A reputation for fecundity was quickly established. The first birth to crofter parents was to John and Anne Campbell in July 1888, and others followed quickly. By the time the census was taken in 1891, Bannatyne and Margaret Mackinnon at Hilton had seen the birth of the last of their ten children; John and Jessie Nicolson had the first of what would be nine children. In all, twenty-six children were born to the crofter settlers during the first two years of settlement. School-age children attended schools at Hilton and Bellafield, and soon developed a fluency in English that most of their parents would never equal.

Though they were never to attract the amount of newspaper attention received by the Saltcoats settlers, the crofters at Pelican Lake were often visited by "observers" during the early years of settlement. Visits are recorded from Sir Charles Tupper in 1889, the ICB's secretary, J.G. Colmer, a Toronto *Globe* correspondent, and certain British farmer delegates sponsored in 1890 by the Canadian government to promote immigration. Michael Davitt, the Irish nationalist, visited Killarney during his tour of Canada and met five family heads in the Lewis settlement. He found Donald MacDonald and Kenneth Macauley content with Manitoba, but John Mackenzie "longed for the sea breeze."[4]

The visit of the tenant farmers from Britain is of particular interest. Eleven years earlier, in 1879, the Canadian government had sponsored a similar visit as a means of generating favourable publicity in Britain to encourage emigration. As negative reports of the Saltcoats crofters' experiences continued to appear in the Scottish press, the Canadian Minister of Agriculture instructed Tupper to issue invitations to representative British farmers to tour the Canadian West during the harvest of 1890. The invitations were to be issued only when a good harvest was assured. The Canadian officials believed that favourable reports by the delegates upon their return to Britain would successfully counter the adverse attention the Canadian West was receiving as a field for immigration. The twelve selected delegates were treated royally in Winnipeg upon their arrival in mid-September. They stayed at the Clarendon Hotel, were made honourary members of the Manitoba Club, and dined with Sir Hector Langevin, Minister of Public Works in Sir John A. Macdonald's government. W.B. Scarth personally conducted a group of the delegates on a visit to the Argyle crofter settlement at Hilton. They visited the homesteads of Roderick Mackay, Donald Mackenzie and Donald Stewart on 24 September 1890. In their reports, published in London in 1891, the delegates stated that, after some initial dissatisfaction, the crofters now had no desire to return to Scotland and that they all told "the same story — prosperity, peace, content[ment]."[5] Interestingly, Scarth did not arrange for a visit to the more troubled Lewis settlement on the other side of Pelican Lake.

The most famous visitors to the crofter colonies arrived just a fortnight after the British farmer delegates. Lord and Lady Aberdeen were actively engaged in emigration work in Scotland and, as part of their Canadian tour in 1890, insisted on personally inquiring into the crofters' circumstances. A special train from Winnipeg brought them to Killarney, and on 8 October, T.J. Lawlor drove them out to the settlements. In private letters to relations in Scotland, Lady Aberdeen described the ride:

> North, south, east, west rolled the illimitable (and detestable) prairies. After 7 or 8 miles we came to the first crofter, one John McLeod, who had been one of the grumblers about small things, but he made no grumble to us and said he thought he

> should get along well now. Then came John Nicolson's section
> (can you conceive of anything more horrid than to have your
> home called Section 1 – 3 – East?).[6]

Nicolson was away from home (actually called SW 25.4.17), but his
visitors admired the 900 bushels of threshed wheat in his new wooden
barn. Visits were also paid to Angus MacLeod, John Mackay, John
Campbell, and Murdo Graham in the Lewis settlement, and to Angus
Morrison and Donald Stewart in the Argyle colony. Unlike the tenant
farmers, Lady Aberdeen certainly did not judge the crofters to be univer-
sally prosperous and content. She and Lawlor, both Liberals in politics,
agreed in their criticisms of Lothian's action in placing penniless fishermen on the prairie too late in the season to get a crop their first year.
Lady Aberdeen stated that the "experiment could scarcely have been
made with more risky people unless it be London paupers."[7] But in contrast to most other commentators, she commended the settlers on their
achievements:

> One requires to think of what these people were before they
> came out, to appreciate their present position and prospects.
> Some who came knew nothing about agricultural work — one
> had never used a hay-fork in his life. And that they should
> have got on so well as they have done is very creditable, both
> to themselves and to their neighbours.[8]

Lady Aberdeen was particularly struck by the solitude of prairie life, de-
scribing the scenery as "inexpressibly dreary" to those raised on Scottish
landscapes. As a result, she organized the Lady Aberdeen Association
for Distributing Literature to Settlers in the West when she returned from
British Columbia to Winnipeg in November. She recruited as her execu-
tive the wives of the heads of prominent land companies (including Mrs.
Scarth) in Winnipeg. This first chapter of the organization, which would
have fifteen branches in Canada by the turn of the century, operated out
of "two nice light airy rooms" in the Land Titles Office. Appeals were
made in Britain, particularly for Scottish newspapers and magazines.
Lady Aberdeen managed to secure a donation from Andrew Carnegie as
well as free freight from the Allan Line and free postage for small-sized
packages from the Canadian post office. The first packages were sent to
settlers in January 1891. Crofters and non-crofters alike would later recall
the joy with which they received *Boys and Girls Own Annuals* and other
literature through the efforts of this association.

To those who could not read English, Lady Aberdeen's charity could
bring no solace. Mary Morrison would often walk the six miles to the
Fairhall Post Office in hopes that there just might be a letter from home.

SALTCOATS: THE FIRST FOUR YEARS

At Saltcoats, the settlers were prevented from becoming the debtors of local merchants. In the summer of 1889, the ICB told the business community that it would refuse to be held responsible for any debt in excess of £120 per family. Though the board subsequently made an additional $3,000 available, the Saltcoats merchants, distinctly free from the illusions of the Killarney business community, extended very little credit to a population already mortgaged beyond the security it could provide. By 1894, when the Saltcoats crofters collectively owed less than $800 to local shopkeepers and implement dealers, the Killarney and Argyle crofters owed more than thirty times that amount.

If the litigation that occurred at Killarney was avoided at Saltcoats, resentment of the crofter settlers was not thereby contained. The crofters settled in an area that was sparsely populated by settlers primarily of British origin. Many of these were assisted settlers of the Commercial Colonisation Company, most were themselves struggling to establish homesteads, and most could offer no employment. In fact, they were competing with the crofters for what few wage opportunities were available. Sir Charles Tupper in 1893 recommended that in future the ICB should settle crofters in groups of no more than six families in order to avoid competition for scarce employment and, more significantly, to prevent the development of a "local prejudice against them."

That a local prejudice existed against the crofters at Saltcoats is supported by fragmentary but highly suggestive evidence. When complaints of overcharging were being investigated, Thomas MacNutt stated that older settlers wished they could claim to be crofters in order to benefit from the low prices at which the crofters were supplied. When complaints that crofters' mail was being tampered with in Canada were being investigated, the postmaster at Saltcoats was certainly displeased at having to defend his integrity. One newspaper report displayed no sympathy for a crofter's frozen feet, preferring to comment on his stupidity in not wearing available footwear. When Knox Presbyterian Church in Winnipeg sent winter clothing to the Saltcoats crofters, another newspaper expressed anger that the clothing had been unnecessarily collected for those already so heavily favoured. The glare of publicity that followed the crofters, particularly until 1891 while the British Committee on Colonisation was hearing evidence, was not appreciated by the local communities. At Saltcoats especially, a steady stream of British and Canadian newspaper correspondents and Scottish travellers was augmented by visits from dignitaries and officials including Colmer, tenant farmer delegations, Department of the Interior officials and ministers, land company commissioners, Sir Charles

Tupper, British MPs, and, on one occasion, Governor-General Lord Stanley accompanied by a ceremonial contingent of Mounted Police. But the Saltcoats correspondent of the *Manitoba Free Press*, as early as October 1889, wrote that the people of the community "do complain of every 'High Muck-a-Muck' coming to Saltcoats to 'visit the Crofters.' Let them visit the Crofter Colonies near Saltcoats if they will."[9] The international celebrities were quickly losing their appreciative local audience.

With the emphatic refusal of the Department of the Interior to bear any responsibility for the crofter colonies, the ICB's Canadian agent assumed the full burden of their day-to-day administration. George Betts Borradaile, the ICB's Crofter Commissioner, was appointed not because he had the confidence of the Department of the Interior and not because the crofters' publicized demand that he be retained had influenced ICB members. Rather, he was appointed because no one else with any familiarity with the Saltcoats situation was available after Grant MacKay was deemed to be unsatisfactory. A member of the North West Mounted Police from 1876 to 1879, Borradaile became a land surveyor in the Territories and, as a Steele Scout, saw action during the Riel Rebellion in 1885. His initial assignment to meet the 1889 party at Halifax was essentially a patronage appointment secured through his brother-in-law, the private secretary to Sir Charles Tupper. With an annual salary of $1,000 plus the keep of a horse, Borradaile was also to receive up to $300 per year for office expenses at Saltcoats and travel expenses to Pelican Lake once or twice a year. By the time his wife joined him from Halifax in late November, he had located on a quarter section in the Lothian Colony and was already preparing the first of the quarterly reports the ICB in London expected from him. He was also attempting to deal with the host of administrative demands for which, in Canada, he was solely responsible. To avoid the necessity and expense of constant communication between Borradaile and London, a Winnipeg-based subcommittee of the ICB would be created within a year. Originally consisting of Henry Hall Smith, Scarth, Eden, and L.A. Hamilton of the CPR, the subcommittee, at no charge, was to play an advisory role to secure the "success of the present experiment, in anticipation of an extension of the colonisation scheme."[10]

During the chaotic summer settlement process, the ICB quickly realized that the funds available to each family were inadequate. At its fourth meeting on 2 July 1889, it reconsidered its earlier decision to refuse advances to family members other than designated family heads. But partly because no funds were made available specifically for this purpose, and partly because nearly all the other family members eligible to enter for a quarter section had left the Saltcoats area by July in search of wages, only four additional entries were made by December 1889. In contrast to Pelican Lake, where ultimately only two eligible males did not take up homesteads, fewer than half the eligible family members were to enter for homesteads at Saltcoats during the life of the colony.

The instructions Borradaile received from the ICB included the warning that the ICB required security for "every cent of the money" advanced to the crofters because the Imperial Treasury would be auditing the accounts. Borradaile's primary responsibility was to look after the interests of the ICB,[11] and it is apparent that both he and his employer did not doubt that this meant the vigilant protection of the securities taken for monies advanced. Though he would advise the settlers on farming practices, he was not, in an agricultural sense, the practical man of the country the ICB claimed him to be. Through the terms of his appointment and, through no fault of his own, he was certainly not the advocate of their interests the settlers initially thought him to be.

The conflicting expectations were clearly revealed during the winter of 1889-90. Delays in planting, drought, and low cash incomes meant that both the Lothian and King colonies required assistance with provisions until a crop could be harvested in the fall of 1890. The ICB knew this and made funds available to Borradaile. No shopkeeper at Saltcoats could extend credit without Borradaile's permission and this permission was not granted until the money required was secured through chattel liens and mortgages. Though this was acceptable to the crofters, a reduction in rations was not. Uncertain that available funds would be enough to support the colonies even until the spring, Borradaile advised settlers and shopkeepers in October of a ration reduction. Citing overrationing and waste, Borradaile stated that a ready market for firewood existed at Saltcoats, thus providing those who found the reduced rations inadequate with the opportunity to earn supplementary income.

The crofters, led by Charles Docherty, argued that work was scarce, complained especially that rations were being denied to any able-bodied person over thirteen years of age, and petitioned Lord Lothian in mid-December. Borradaile, informed by Colmer on 15 January 1890 of the complaints, responded aggressively. He told the crofters that all rations would cease on 20 March. He wrote to Colmer stating that he was attempting to minimize costs and emphasizing that "the only way to render these people self supporting is to deny their right to any supplies." A.F. Eden was asked to investigate the petitioners' complaints. He admitted that work was scarce, but advised Henry Hall Smith that he agreed completely with Borradaile's policy on rationing. However, before this endorsement reached the ICB, reports appeared in the Toronto newspapers that the crofter communities in the Northwest were suffering from destitution and starvation. The charges were quickly repeated in the Scottish newspapers, questions were asked in the British Parliament, and Sir Charles Tupper postponed a trip to the Italian Riviera to attend an emergency ICB meeting in London on 25 February. When a series of letters from the Saltcoats crofters cataloguing their complaints appeared in the Inverness *Scottish Highlander*, the ICB found itself involved in a considerable controversy. Borradaile, chastised for having failed to anticipate the situation, cabled that destitution rumours were "exaggerated," though he admitted children's clothing would be welcome. A letter signed by Docherty and fifteen other Saltcoats crofters was published in the *Highlander* stating that on 14 April Borradaile reaffirmed that no more provisions would be provided even though only ten days' supplies remained to them.

The situation was desperate, but Borradaile had not been idle. In mid-May, he proudly advised Colmer that he had "sent" ten family heads from the King Colony and four from the Lothian Colony to work at Rat Portage where he had personally secured employment for them.[12] Evidence later provided by Colmer to the Select Committee on Colonisation and records of the Scottish Office reflect no disapproval of the stern, paternalistic approach adopted by their Canadian agent. For its part, the ICB, at its 25 February emergency meeting, decided to approach what it knew would be an irate Treasury with a request for £500 for "extra maintenance" to provide for the Saltcoats settlers until the harvest of 1890. Additional funding was also required immediately for seed grain. Lothian and Tupper, recognizing that the Treasury could not be approached yet again, made personal appeals that the Saltcoats crofters be provided with seed grain under the Canadian scheme resulting from the 1889 drought. The Department of the Interior, reluctant because the crofters' lands were already mortgaged to the legal limit, finally agreed, placed liens upon the anticipated crops and provided the seed on 2 April.

Textual extracts and the statistical portion of Borradaile's first annual report were published as appendices to the second ICB report. Though offering criticisms of the agricultural habits of his wards at Saltcoats, Borradaile expressed the opinion that the crop of 1890 "had made hopeful North-West farmers of them all." He anticipated a substantial increase in land being broken for 1891, and noted that a few settlers had jointly purchased farm implements and that most families had secured some cash income during the summer and fall. He could not conceal his dismay, however, that thirteen of the fourteen family heads sent to work in May refused to return for the harvest. Preferring the uncertainties of casual labour to the uncertainties of prairie farming, they had been joined by their own families and by three other King Colony families, leaving only a recent widow and her family in the King Colony. Less than eighteen months after it was founded, the King Colony ceased to exist. The ICB, perplexed by this development, appended to its second report a letter from one of the tenant farmer delegates of 1890 which indicated that "men with a moderate amount of brains and energy" could accomplish a great deal in Canada.[13] The not-so-subtle implication was that the Saltcoats crofters were lacking in both respects. Clearly, the political battles in Scotland were still being fought, and this would not be the last time the emigrant crofters themselves would be blamed for problems with the settlement scheme. Borradaile, taking security, distributed what he could of the abandoned goods and chattels amongst the eleven other family members who had taken out homesteads by the end of 1890, and sold the rest to other Saltcoats-area residents. The ICB took possession of the abandoned quarter sections and wrote to the Canadian Department of the Interior forcefully requesting legislation "of a restrictive character" to prevent settlers from abandoning obligations to their sponsor in such a "free and easy fashion."[14]

The fall of 1890 also witnessed the visits to the crofter colonies of two British MPs in search of support for their own views on emigration issues. Sir George Baden-Powell, a member of the Select Committee on Colonisation and a supporter of the Lothian scheme, arrived at Killarney in early October at the same time as Lord and Lady Aberdeen were investigating conditions there. Sir George did not interview any of the settlers, spoke only to the shopkeepers, and returned to England to testify before the Committee that the scheme was good, but the settlers bad. G.B Clark, also a Committee member but an adamant opponent of crofter emigration, went directly to Saltcoats in late October to enquire into the settlement scandals there. He caused much confusion in the colony by claiming that seed grain was to be supplied at Imperial government expense. He listened to the crofter complaints, asked them to document their case, and returned to England with a bitter document signed by a group led by Charles Docherty. The document was a catalogue of broken promises and mistreatment. The signatories criticized Colmer's conduct during his visit of the previous year, and referred to Borradaile as "an unclean thing" among them.

As long as he remained Crofter Commissioner, Borradaile was hard pressed to repeat even the strained optimism regarding the Saltcoats settlements that he projected in his first report. An unusually high incidence of deaths and illnesses occurred. By the end of 1893, seven adults and two children were dead; two women were in asylums, and several cases of chronic illness were causing serious concern. Other deaths, especially of adult males, were to follow, adding to the troubles of the beleaguered colony. Some widows and families joined those who had abandoned and gone to Rat Portage or Selkirk; others went to relatives at Pelican Lake or Moosomin. Remaining families took what comfort they could from the births of their first Canadian-born children. The census of 1891 indicates that twelve children were born to the remaining colonists during the first two years of settlement.

Though the 1890 crop was sharply reduced by harvest rains and improper stacking, it provided sufficient income to pay store debts and, for the first time, to sustain the settlers during the approaching winter. The 1891 crop was severely damaged by a local frost in late August. The crop of 1892 was partially devastated by hot winds and electrical storms, and a discouraged crofter population allowed livestock to forage over what remained. As a result, Borradaile was obliged to request renewed assistance in the purchase of seed grain; the ICB demurred and though it did finally sanction the expenditure for seed grain, at least one crofter felt that the grain arrived too late and fed it to his cattle. Discouraged by the succession of poor seasons, and deterred by the low prices prevailing in the early 1890s, many of the crofters determined that livestock were more suited to the area than grain and reduced their acreage under cultivation after 1892. Others, despairing that any form of farming could allow the repayment of their loans, simply abandoned their homesteads. In the autumn of 1892, only eighteen heads and thirteen other family members remained on their homesteads. Ironically, not one had acquired the pre-emption — the issue that so urgently occupied Tupper and the Scottish Office at the time of settlement — by the end of their third year on the land. By the autumn of 1893, only twenty-three settlers remained.

ADMINISTRATION AND POLITICS

Throughout this period, Borradaile engaged in a constant preparation of accounts and correspondence with Colmer regarding accounts and accounting practices. Unexplained or missing vouchers, unauthorized expenditures, and even discrepancies of a few cents invariably resulted in the Scottish Office demanding explanations and revisions from Colmer. As ICB secretary, Colmer found himself constantly berating Borradaile for imprecision and tardiness while trying to placate a Scottish Office attempting to meet Treasury deadlines. The transfer of abandoned goods and chattels to the remaining Saltcoats settlers in 1890 caused considerable dismay about legal and financial proprieties at the Scottish Office; accounts submitted by Borradaile in February 1892 required five months' correspondence before being submitted to the Treasury in July. Borradaile was regularly reminded that his responsibility was primarily that of a financial custodian.

Though Borradaile was never to satisfy his employer in that respect, the crofter settlers at Saltcoats perceived him as enforcing his instructions almost ruthlessly. After removing to Winnipeg in the summer of 1892, Borradaile found it necessary to engage a "subagent" to carry out his instructions at the Saltcoats settlement, and ironically his former neighbour, crofter Charles Docherty, agreed to act in this capacity. For the first year of settlement, Docherty had been the organizer and spokesman of crofter grievances. Yet when the tenant farmer delegates visited him in September 1890, he told them he would not leave the country unless he were "dragged away with ropes." Docherty's duties as subagent included taking charge of abandoned animals and securing lumber from abandoned homesteads, as well as legally restraining the other crofters from acting against the interests of the ICB. In the winter of 1892-93, that restraint entailed threatening to arrest for larceny any crofter selling the natural increase from ICB livestock without express permission. Borradaile felt that the natural increase belonged to the ICB and added to its security. The crofters felt that their livestock were the only possessions they had which the ICB did not own. Alexander Young sued Docherty in a related dispute over oxen.

The widespread resentment against Borradaile was forcefully expressed in a petition addressed to the new Secretary for Scotland, Sir George Trevelyan, on 31 May 1893. With twenty signatures, the petition sought relocation of the signatories on better lands and was accompanied by individual statements alleging mistreatment by the climate and by Borradaile. Organized by the school teacher, Colin Macleay, the petitioners sought redress of grievances dating back to their arrival at Halifax on 14 April 1889.[15] However, eight settlers who supported Docherty did not sign the petition. The settlement was sharply divided and again apparently in turmoil. As a result, Sir Charles Tupper was asked to investigate the complaints during his visit to Canada on private business during the autumn of 1893. In another petition to Trevelyan, members of Macleay's faction announced their complete lack of confidence in Tupper's objectivity and stated that work pressures would prevent them from seeing him during his visit.

Borradaile, not without complaint, provided the ICB with detailed rebuttals of every charge against him. This served to confirm the impression Tupper had formed through interviews with him during his Canadian visit. Tupper offered no criticism whatsoever of the Canadian agent and quite correctly concluded that Borradaile was acting with complete integrity in protecting the ICB's interests. Equally, he pointed out that many complaints had been gone over thoroughly in testimony before the

Colonisation Committee in 1890 and 1891, that some of the recent petitioners denied the truth of assertions made in the petition, and that Colin
Macleay sought to replace Borradaile as the ICB's agent. Curiously though,
Tupper thereby characterized the complaints as having "little or no foun-
dation" and concluded that the scheme could not "in any way be described
as a failure."[16] In his written report to the Secretary for Scotland, he stated
that Macleay was the source of all the problems at Saltcoats. He even urged
the ICB to use its influence to prevent Macleay's teaching contract from being renewed by the Territorial government. Macleay, like Docherty before
him, saw his opinions discredited and his character disparaged for press-
ing the Saltcoats crofters' case "too forcefully." Yet between signing the
petition in May and Tupper's visit in mid-September, four signatories
abandoned their homesteads — "surreptitiously" according to a chagrined
Borradaile — and one died. Of the twenty-four settlers remaining, Tupper
spoke personally to ten during his brief visit to Saltcoats; only three gave
him good accounts of the Northwest. John McKay told Tupper bluntly,
"We should never have come."

The first four years' experience of the crofters near Saltcoats had certainly been grim. More than half of the forty-nine families had
abandoned their homesteads and had left the area. The Superintendent
of the Presbyterian Church at Winnipeg twice found it necessary to appeal for donations of clothing. The first public appeal in February 1890
had resulted in an uproar in the press in both Scotland and Canada. The
second appeal, conducted without publicity through Knox Presbyterian
Church in Winnipeg, occurred during the bitterly cold February of 1892.
When the North West Mounted Police of the Saltcoats detachment expressed concern in 1893 at the dire poverty of one family in particular,
they were informed by Borradaile that the ICB was not a charitable insti-
tution. As the dry years of the early 1890s unfolded, the land itself
seemed to provide only bitter harvests and empty dreams.

At Pelican Lake, the settlements initiated in 1888 and developed along
different lines provided better support for Tupper's positive judgement
of the colonization scheme. It is important to note that Borradaile's status
amongst the Pelican Lake settlers was always that of an occasional visitor
on official business; he was not, even temporarily as at Saltcoats, a resident amongst the people he administered. The date of Borradaile's first
visit is unrecorded, though it is possible he accompanied Colmer in October 1889. The ICB's intention was that its agent should visit once or twice
a year to report on progress and, eventually, to collect repayment installments. With seed grain provided through the municipality by the
provincial government, the Pelican Lake crofters harvested their first

satisfactory crops in the autumn of 1890. This performance was repeated in 1891 and in 1892, though prices remained severely depressed. The ICB's reports for these years indicated, with an obvious delight, ever-increasing figures for acreage under cultivation, crop production, and livestock possession. Though minor individual differences were indicated, both the Killarney and Argyle portions of the settlement were shown to be sharing equally in the progress. Low agricultural prices and poor agricultural practices were regularly cited by Borradaile as inhibiting the settlers' progress, but the consensus of the agent and the ICB was that progress was gratifying and that the Imperial funds were well-secured.

However, severe difficulties existed due to the amount of external debt owed by the crofters to local shopkeepers and implement dealers. Henry Hall Smith's first report hinted that unauthorized debts had been incurred even as the crofters were being settled in 1888. The Killarney merchant, T.J. Lawlor, wrote to Smith about store debts in June 1889. In his first report, Borradaile expressed concern at the "weighty obligations" undertaken to acquire farm machinery. In his 1891 report, he advised the ICB of the precise debts of each crofter to the implement agents. Only fifteen of the thirty-nine "other" family members were free from these obligations. Each of the family heads was in debt to implement dealers, with obligations ranging from a low of $106 to John Nicolson's debt of $415; the total debt to implement dealers was $8,779.56. Attention shifted to debts for taxes and seed grain advances when, in September 1892, thirty-five properties were nominally seized by the municipality and offered for sale. The average debt for these properties was $34 and totalled nearly $1,200. As part of his report for 1893, Borradaile included individual statements of debts to the ICB, the municipalities, the shopkeepers, and the implement dealers. External debts were shown to exceed, by over $1,000, the $23,799.37 that was collectively owed to the ICB. Five years after their arrival, the Pelican Lake colonists were in debt for nearly $50,000.[17]

In 1894, the *Fifth Report of the Imperial Colonisation Board* made public the extent of the indebtedness at Pelican Lake, but was distinctly reticent about related financial detail. The longstanding dispute over settlement expenditures with the CNWL had finally been resolved. The land company reluctantly assumed responsibility for nearly $2,000 advanced without authorization from the Scottish Office, and accepted a reduced sum on other expense claims. Since the land exchange between the CNWL and the Canadian government had also been formally sanctioned in October 1890, the ICB, three years after the settlement at Pelican Lake, took legal possession of the liens against fifty-five properties. The CNWL retained possession of thirteen properties assigned primarily to other family members of the Harris contingent. The *Fifth Report* did not state that the debt figures applied only to the settlers for whom the ICB held security and did not include the thirteen CNWL properties. The average debt of the thirty family heads, exclusive of interest on the Imperial advance, was also not stated in the report. According to Borradaile's figures, it was $1,272.20 in December 1893.

Tupper was concerned. He wrote to Trevelyan that

> the Crofters have burdened themselves with a lot of machinery which they ought not to have had, and they have run up debts at the stores which they should never have incurred, and have had, of course, to give mortgages on their crops in order to meet their indebtedness.[18]

But nowhere in his reports does Tupper suggest that the extension of credit could have been precisely what the progress and prosperity was based upon and that, without it, the Pelican Lake settlements could not have survived. Eventually, creditors must be paid. Even as Tupper was in Winnipeg in September 1893, at least five new legal actions were in progress in Killarney to secure proceeds from the crops of individual crofters. Before he had received Borradaile's December report, Tupper recommended to Trevelyan that, for reasons quite distinct from those that applied at Saltcoats, the Pelican Lake settlers should not be pressed to begin repayment of Imperial funds for "a year or two." Though they were prosperous, he regarded their prosperity as fragile. At both Saltcoats and Pelican Lake, therefore, what was regarded as the only true measure of the settlement scheme's success or failure — namely, repayment — was to be postponed.

By the autumn of 1893, several indications were apparent of how Lothian's scheme was being judged in various quarters. The British Select Committee on Colonisation, after two full years of hearing evidence, had finally reported in March 1891. While the Committee was more enthusiastic about the New Zealand and British Columbia proposals for crofter colonization, it recommended that parliamentary funds should be made available for "a moderately numerous party" of crofters to emigrate to the Northwest under the auspices of the ICB. It warned, however, that false expectations amongst prospective emigrants should be strictly guarded against, and further recommended that the congested districts of Ireland should also benefit from such a scheme.[19] Lothian welcomed this qualified endorsement. The ICB was duly reconstituted to include Irish members, and in June 1892 Parliament voted £7,500 for the use of the expanded ICB. The ICB made plans to spend £300 in the autumn to break ten acres per family in the Oxbow district of the North-West Territories, and applications were invited in August from crofter families in Scotland who were advised to expect an advance of up to £150 upon embarkation in March 1893. Apparently the fundamental lessons of 1888 and 1889 had been well learned.

For unknown reasons, the Canadian government delayed the designation of a reserve of land in the Oxbow region and, when the townships were finally chosen, Borradaile judged them to be unsuitable "to the requirements of settlers of so little knowledge and experience of farming as the average Crofter."[20] In his final month in office, Lothian was denied the services of Malcolm McNeill for family selections by the always reluctant Edinburgh Board of Supervision. Though sufficient numbers of applications had been received from the Highlands, the Orkneys, and the Shetlands, the new Secretary for Scotland delayed consideration of the matter until the ICB's thirteenth meeting on 16 May 1893. Trevelyan, unlike Lothian, was apparently not in a hurry to transfer crofter families to the Canadian West. His decision not to proceed with the proposed emigration of 1893 was based upon the fact that, as the ICB sadly admitted in its *Fourth Report*, no applications had been received "from families in the districts from which the settlers at Killarney and Saltcoats came."[21] If Sir Charles Tupper did not understand John McKay's message, the islands of Lewis and Harris had heard it clearly. On a visit to the Western Isles in April 1893, Colin Scott-Moncrieff, the new Under-Secretary for Scotland, reported that Lothian's 1892 posters were never seen in Lewis and that six Saltcoats families had returned to the Long Island.

The Winnipeg subcommittee, perhaps in an attempt to influence the ICB's May meeting, resigned *en masse* on 27 April, arguing that, with no further immigration planned, there would be no purpose for it to serve. Tupper was able to revive the subcommittee on his September visit, but it ceased to play a significant intermediary and advisory role to either Borradaile or to the ICB. After his return from Saltcoats, Tupper was embarrassed by reports in the Winnipeg papers of Trevelyan's statement to Parliament that the crofter colonisation scheme was an utter failure. Trevelyan added:

> I believe that the people who were sent out were not natural emigrants; and not only so, but that when they had energy and self-reliance, they were so cockered up under this system that they lost it.[22]

Although Trevelyan was not a champion of the crofting community, neither did he see his constituency as including the landed interests associated with Lothian. Gladstonian principles of *laissez-faire* had returned to the Scottish Office. With no financial evidence of the success of Lothian's scheme before him, Trevelyan declared that public funds could not have been worse spent, refused to hold an ICB meeting specifically to consider the results of Tupper's inquiry, and arranged for an early presentation to Parliament of the bleak *Fourth Report of the Imperial Colonisation Board.*

CHAPTER FIVE

Settlements and Administration to 1906

THE ANNOUNCEMENT that the British government would countenance no more assistance to emigration schemes had no effect whatsoever on the ICB's administration of its Canadian settlements. Though differences emerged between the Scottish and Canadian interests amongst ICB members, the fulfillment of financial obligations to the British Treasury remained the primary consideration. The collection of debt repayments from the settlers was, therefore, the focus of the ICB's actions and deliberations after 1894. The ICB found itself in an adversarial position with its settlers (especially those at Killarney), with creditors of the settlers, and increasingly even with its own Canadian agent. After some hesitation, it imposed a change in its legal relationship to the settlers in 1897-98, which at the same time established the paramountcy of its own claims over those of all other creditors. The return to power of a Conservative government in Britain in 1895 entailed no renewed interest in colonization, and by the end of the century, the perfunctory ICB reports reflected a desire to wind up the Commission's affairs. After 1894, no government-assisted emigration from the congested districts of Scotland or Ireland was even contemplated.

LIABILITIES AND LITIGATION

The numbers of notable people visiting the colonies after the first few years fell dramatically. No longer did the residents of Saltcoats find it possible to complain of "High Muck-a-Mucks" visiting the crofters: after Tupper in 1893, the only visits recorded are those by Borradaile. At Pelican Lake too, apart from Borradaile's annual visits and the appearance of an occasional British MP, the crofter settlers found that they were no longer in the public spotlight. In the autumn of 1893, another delegation of British tenant farmers visited the Killarney area as guests of the Canadian government. They found the crofters deeply concerned about debt and anxious about their future. Many of the uncertainties of 1888 were apparently unresolved five years later.

Even the Scottish Office was confused about repayment of the government advances. In two respects, the liens taken by the CNWL in 1888 proved to be illegal under the *Dominion Lands Act*. Whereas Lothian's scheme and the liens taken under it required repayments to begin in July

1892 after four years on the land, the Canadian legislation provided for repayments at the end of the fifth year after settlement, and prohibited collection until after the harvest. The Canadian government passed amending legislation in May 1889 permitting repayment to begin after four years. A frantic exchange of letters between the ICB, the Scottish Office, and the Treasury occurred from June to November 1892 in an attempt to answer legal questions and establish the terms upon which repayments could be expected. Treasury officials severely chastised the Scottish Office for launching a scheme in such haste that its provisions did not accord with Dominion law, and pointed out that even the interest rate upon which it had based its calculations was incorrect. Payments were initially due from the Pelican Lake family heads on 1 July 1892, and from other family members on 1 November 1892. From family heads and other members at Saltcoats, the dates were 1 November 1893 and 1 November 1894 respectively.

All dates passed with Borradaile being unable to collect any repayments except from one younger man at Killarney.[1] The Treasury expressed its extreme disapproval that the Parliament-approved scheme had been so widely departed from, and that so little effort had been expended in the pursuit of collections. In his defence, Borradaile stated that he had visited Killarney three times for collection purposes and had sent four notices to each debtor "explaining in a lucid manner the amount due." As early as 18 March 1893, he urged the ICB to consider legal action to compel payment, stating that some of the Pelican Lake settlers clearly had the ability to pay. It was recognized that the remaining Saltcoats settlers possessed no comparable ability and their failure to meet repayment deadlines was viewed with more indulgence by both Borradaile and the ICB.

It must be emphasized that the abandonment of plans for further emigration resulted in no change in the ICB's administrative policies. The ICB continued to see the protection of investment and the recovery of debt as its sole mandate. Behind this unity in policy, however, lay a division of purpose. Trevelyan sought the retrieval of Imperial funds in order to formally end the colonization experiment and to dissolve the ICB. The Under-Secretary for Scotland, Colin Scott-Moncrieff, who was also a member of the ICB after August 1893, agreed but continued to see emigration as the only solution to the problems of the congested crofting parishes. Sir Charles Tupper sought a successful conclusion in order to encourage at least an increased private emigration to the Canadian Northwest, if not a renewed interest in government assistance to emigrants. As secretary to both the High Commissioner's Office and the ICB,

Colmer was ideally placed to assist Tupper in this, particularly as the responsibility for the preparation of the Board's annual reports was his.

Tupper was able to convince his fellow ICB members that the settlers should not be pressed for immediate repayment. The annual reports, issued in June 1894 and April 1895, certainly criticized the settlers for failing to meet financial obligations, but offered adverse weather conditions, severely depressed agricultural prices and even primitive agricultural practices, as explanations for that failure. The ICB, to the evident annoyance of Borradaile, did not join the Killarney merchants in repossessing chattels or in resorting to legal action to compel payments. T.J. Lawlor told the Scottish Office that without reducing principal amounts, the 1894 crop "was largely consumed in defraying bailiff's fees and court costs," and said the 1895 crop would meet the same fate.[2]

The Treasury insisted that the indulgence should cease. After six years of expressing dissatisfaction with the ICB's accounting practices, the Treasury finally intervened to dictate policy in March 1895. It authorized the ICB to pay the overdue taxes on the thirty-five properties at Killarney, and it insisted that the crofters be advised that they would lose their homesteads unless municipal tax, seed grain accounts, and "some portion of the instalment due to the Board" were paid by November 1895. All homesteads of other family members were to revert to the ICB unless two years' installments had been paid by that date; proceedings were to be launched against selected family heads. Continuing the more lenient treatment of the Saltcoats settlers, proceedings there were to be launched only where a "*bona fide* attempt" to meet obligations had not been made. Essentially, Borradaile's 1893 recommendations were to be acted upon in 1895. The difficulty in adopting a common policy derived from the fact that circumstances varied widely at the three remaining colonies. Because those circumstances were to diverge even more sharply after 1895, each settlement warrants separate consideration.

THE LOTHIAN COLONY

In recognition of a succession of disastrous agricultural seasons and due to ongoing discomfort over the settlement fiasco in 1889, the ICB continued to treat the Lothian Colony at Saltcoats with a degree of indulgence it did not extend to the Argyle and Killarney settlements. In 1895, under instructions from the ICB, Borradaile personally advised the fourteen family heads and the eight other family members still resident on their homesteads of the ICB's intentions. By this time, the settlers were practically debt free apart from their obligations to the ICB, having continued to earn wages where possible and having achieved some success in rearing livestock. The twenty-two remaining settlers had practically the same acreage prepared for cultivation in 1896 as they had in 1890, but had substantially increased their livestock and poultry. The response of the settlers to the ICB's demands was a humble and judiciously worded request, transmitted to the ICB through the office of its agent, that they be given permission to abandon their homesteads. Basically, their proposal was that the ICB should accept their properties as payment of debts, while the settlers would be permitted to enter for new homesteads further north of Saltcoats in an area more conducive to stock-rearing. The ICB, at its seventeenth meeting on 29 November 1895, directed Tupper to request the Canadian government to comply with Borradaile's recommendation that these second homesteads be permitted, but only if the settlers gave liens to the ICB for the difference in value between the amount owed and the assessed value of each original homestead. Pending a decision by Canadian authorities, legal proceedings launched on 2 November against all Saltcoats crofters were suspended.

In the interests of "general emigration work," Tupper strongly urged the Minister of the Interior to allow the crofters' proposal. As in all previous matters concerning the settlement scheme, the Canadian authorities acted slowly and inefficiently. Colmer urged a quick decision in February 1896 lest another year be lost. The Department of the Interior advised the ICB of its general approval of the idea, but announced delays in formalities in March and September. Another enquiry by Colmer in February 1897 finally resulted in legislation by the new Laurier government in July. The Saltcoats settlers were told by Borradaile that they would have to leave their homesteads by the following spring. But the legislation required an evaluation by the Department of the Interior of the first homesteads before their abandonment, and by January 1898 this had still not occurred. By the end of 1897, seven more settlers (including Charles Docherty and his son) had simply abandoned their homesteads. The ICB regretted that not one settler would agree to take advantage of the legislation passed specifically for them and began again to talk of protecting the ICB's interests at Saltcoats.

THE ARGYLE SETTLEMENT

The ninety-five individuals settled in the Argyle district northeast of Pelican Lake had distinguished themselves from the Lewis settlers by consistently avoiding involvement in petitions, by not requiring seed grain assistance in 1890, and by acquiring substantially smaller debt loads than their neighbours nearer Killarney. Their proximity to the railroad at Hilton had given them a distinct economic advantage. After the settlement with the CNWL, the ICB held the mortgages on only fifteen properties belonging to twelve family heads and three other family members. None of these properties was seized for non-payment of taxes in 1893. Two of the three properties belonging to the other family members had no external debt recorded against them. One family head had no external debt and was reported to be lending money at interest to neighbours. Borradaile urged that no leniency be shown the moneylender, and early in 1895, proceedings were launched against him.[3] However, none of the others had paid their debt installments, and on 2 November, foreclosure proceedings were launched against the other fourteen property holders. By March 1897 all had agreed to the ICB's terms and had signed the necessary leases.

The course of action adopted by the ICB was entirely consistent with the fiscal requirements of the Treasury. At the same time, it was not a Draconian attempt to dispossess the crofters of their Canadian homesteads. The ICB, as landlord, was to collect annual rent payments from its "tenants." When, after eight years, those payments equalled the debt to the ICB, title to the property was to revert to the settlers. Because rent formed a "first charge" upon the land after taxes under Manitoba law, there is no doubt this system recommended itself to the ICB as one through which ICB claims took precedence over those of other creditors. The system was adopted smoothly in the Argyle district and postponed at Saltcoats. The reaction of the Killarney settlers contrasted sharply with those of their fellow crofters and was, typically, overtly political.

THE KILLARNEY SETTLEMENT

Advised in April 1895 of the ICB's intentions should the November payments not be received, the Killarney crofters by mid-May had forwarded lengthy and highly literate petitions to the Secretary for Scotland and, for the first time, to the Manitoba government. It must be remembered that ownership of land had been the chief inducement that persuaded the crofters to come to Manitoba. To return to a landless position and to a tenant status would be a bitter pill to swallow. Arguing that circumstances of settlement, climate, and agricultural necessity had combined to create a position of indebtedness over which the settlers had no control, the petitions sought a satisfactory resolution to the payment of external debt and the placement of a "resident agent" at Killarney. The Scottish Office and Colmer firmly believed that the Killarney merchants had instigated the petition. The document was prepared at the office of a Killarney attorney, and both Lawlor and Finlay Young, the local MLA, were present at a later crofter meeting. The Manitoba government advised the Scottish Secretary that it endorsed the petition and offered its assistance in selecting a suitable agent; without advising British authorities, it then provided $400 from the provincial treasury for a crofter delegation to visit London in support of the petition.[4] The Manitoba government became involved because it was concerned that, if the crofters were turned out of their homes, they might become public charges.

On 2 November, the Killarney settlers were issued notice of the ICB's foreclosure proceedings. With provincial funding secured, they met on 30 January 1896 at Bellafield School and, with T.J. Lawlor as secretary and Finlay Young in attendance, elected John Nicolson and Allan Morrison, a Manitoba College student-missionary, as their delegates to London. The meeting generated yet another petition which was conveyed to London by the delegates in early March 1896. The ICB did not call a meeting to hear the delegation. Instead, Nicolson and Morrison had a private interview with Lord Balfour of Burleigh, who had been appointed Secretary for Scotland in the new Salisbury administration and had therefore become the chairman of the ICB in mid-1895. The delegates presented their case, and the Secretary for Scotland seriously considered recommending that the ICB should assume the external debt. Local interest rates at Killarney, the delegates claimed, were in the range of 12 to 24 percent, and some crofters were without resources to purchase seed grain for the coming season. Borradaile confirmed that livestock was being repossessed and that some settlers had no credit with which to obtain seed grain. John Nicolson, described by Borradaile as "without exception the best crofter assisted by the Board," so impressed the Secretary for Scotland that he appointed him to head a crofter committee to distribute the required seed grain assistance. After making a series of allegations against the ICB's Canadian agent, the delegates returned to Killarney in late March, confident of having created in London a renewed sympathy with the settlement's difficulties.

Through another series of misunderstandings amongst Nicolson, Balfour, Borradaile, and Colmer over the distribution of the seed grain a great deal of ill will occurred, though the twenty-one settlers who received the assistance expressed their gratitude by writing to the Scottish Office. Borradaile's written response to the complaints made against him by Nicolson and Morrison in London drew from the Scottish Office the rare assertion that he "had done his work well, and has had a most unsatisfactory set of men to deal with."[5] If Borradaile's reputation was rising at the Scottish Office, it diminished even further amongst the Killarney crofters when he insisted that the responsibility for seed-grain distribution was his alone. Nicolson disagreed and was also surprised to learn that foreclosure notices had been served on all family heads during his absence. He received one himself upon his arrival in Winnipeg from England. He wrote to Balfour demanding to know why he had not been told of this development while he was in London. As the dispute became more bitter, Nicolson made further allegations against Borradaile and advised the Scottish Office that the crofters wished the ICB to understand that they had not come to Canada "to feed a whole herd of Solicitors." Accusations and counteraccusations were exchanged until, by December 1896, Nicolson had lost all credibility with ICB officials. Balfour decided that an independent inquiry should be launched, and in February 1897, the Treasury approved the expenditure of £200 for this purpose.

Before the inquiry was undertaken, the ICB received news that another crofter delegation, again financed by the Manitoba government, and this time comprised of Nicolson and Lawlor, was en route to London. Borradaile had telegraphed that sixteen Killarney crofters, under advice from Lawlor and Nicolson, refused to sign the leases. But the special ICB meeting convened on 17 May 1897 heard from a sharply divided delegation. Lawlor and Nicolson agreed only that harvest profits were being seized by creditors without overall debts being appreciably diminished. Lawlor presented Killarney merchants' accounts totalling nearly $38,000 including interest and legal fees, and an offer to settle for seventy-five cents on the dollar. Nicolson disputed the merchants' claims, challenged the necessity of the legal costs involved in the foreclosures, and asked a series of questions concerning Borradaile's instructions and legal authority. The only effect the representations had was to add to the list of issues to be investigated by John Rankine, the Edinburgh University professor appointed to inquire into the position and prospects of the ICB's settlers.

Professor Rankine arrived at Winnipeg on 9 August 1897 and stayed in the West until 28 August. He met with Borradaile, Stewart Tupper (who represented the ICB's solicitors), and all the crofters at Pelican Lake except Catherine Mackinnon and Samuel Graham. Rankine also held two long meetings with the creditors of the crofters at a Winnipeg hotel. His lengthy and detailed report was received by the ICB in October. Though the report acknowledged that ill feelings against Borradaile were firmly held by a few Killarney crofters, Rankine endorsed the agent's actions on every point at issue, stating that any mistake he had made "was the outcome of zeal in the service of the Board." Rankine wrote that the settlers who refused to sign the lease (now reduced to fourteen in number) all claimed that high external debts would make them unable to make high annual lease payments. He regretted that the ICB's offer to collect external debt at the rate of fifty cents on the dollar had ultimately been rejected by the creditors.[6] T.J. Lawlor, by far the largest creditor, led the opposition to the proposal. (Of the $37,988.15 claimed, Lawlor's claim was $16,491.48.) After a meeting of all creditors with Rankine in

Winnipeg, Lawlor wrote to the Deputy Minister of the Interior urging Clifford Sifton, Minister of the Interior in Laurier's government, to intervene to convince Rankine that the proposed "settlement" of 20 to 50 percent was "not at all in line with inducements, or what the creditors were led to hope for." Clearly, Lawlor was referring to the visit of Henry Hall Smith to Killarney ten years earlier. He characterized Borradaile as a political foe of the Liberal party, and asked:

> How can Sir Donald Smith [Tupper's successor as Canadian High Commissioner in London] continue to advocate further immigration schemes when he has a colony of his own flesh and blood apt at any moment to transplant themselves across the boundary line?[7]

The Treasury in Britain subsequently approved the ICB's proposed collection scheme. Though all other creditors wanted to accept the plan, Lawlor and F.S. Moule (also of Killarney) rejected it. They convinced other creditors to demand an immediate payment of sixty cents on the dollar on all debts outstanding. Without Lawlor's consent, no agreement was possible and the ICB could report no resolution when it issued its *Ninth Report* in December 1898.

At the same time, the ICB reported that all Killarney crofters had finally signed the required leases. And for the crofters, there was at last some good news. The amount collectively owed by the Killarney and Argyle settlers to the British Treasury was to be reduced by over $9,200, a sum representing the accrued interest on the original advances; the ICB also agreed to pay 50 percent of the legal costs of the foreclosure proceedings, a reduction valued at nearly $2,000. Increasing legal pressure and the substantial easing of terms had reduced the number of holdouts, and when the ICB launched eviction proceedings in July 1898, Nicolson and his six remaining followers reluctantly signed the leases though they were forced to pay the full legal costs.

The process had been bitter. Borradaile, very much the ICB's agent, had won no new friends amongst the crofters or the Killarney merchants. The alliance of merchants and crofters *vis-à-vis* the ICB had been shattered as the ICB asserted that its own financial interests preceded all others. The struggle had not gone unnoticed by the local community. Early in 1897, an appeal for funds to aid in the construction of a Gaelic church at Bellafield caused the new local weekly, *The Killarney Guide*, to print an article on the evils of assisted immigration as well as a letter from "A Canadian," probably an anonymous Killarney merchant, stating that crofters "lack pluck and industry, as well as truthfulness and honesty; it can be proven right here in Killarney or Bellafield... [T]hey are neither willing or [sic] able to pay their debts."[8] Reporting on one of Borradaile's visits, the newspaper sarcastically described the crofters as "the chosen people." In the midst of this hostility, the Killarney crofters constructed their stone church at Bellafield — a solid symbol of their intention to remain.

If the ICB believed that the landlord-tenant arrangements would of themselves facilitate debt collection, it was immediately forced to revise that opinion in November 1898 when collections amounted to virtually nothing. The Canadian climate was not subject to legal regulation, and snow and rain severely reduced crops in both the Killarney and Argyle settlements. Nevertheless, Borradaile reported that five settlers had purchased additional lands while claiming an inability to pay the first installments under their lease agreements, and argued the necessity of legal action against all forty-one of the settlers who had failed to fulfill their lease requirements. The legal threats appear to have had the desired effect. By 31 March 1899, Borradaile was able to report the collection of nearly $3,000 in lease installments. He asked for and received discretionary legal power to enforce the terms of the lease agreements without seeking prior ICB approval for each separate legal action.

Under the power of attorney he received, in 1899 Borradaile appointed a "watchman" at Pelican Lake in the belief that some of the crofters intended "to dispose of their crops and chattels to the prejudice of the Board."[9] The Scottish Office was aghast at the expense ($112.50) and the impropriety of the appointment. This unauthorized step was justified by Colmer as further evidence of the agent's zeal on the ICB's behalf and was forgiven due to an impressive annual lease collection totalling over $4,700 to 30 March 1900. Grain prices in the Killarney area had begun to improve in 1896 and by 1897 briefly regained their 1888 levels. After 1897, prices remained firm at fifty-five to sixty cents per bushel. During the period when the leases were in effect, the amounts collected each year were necessarily dependent upon agricultural production, with the poor harvests of 1900 and 1903 resulting in considerable ICB-initiated litigation or threat of litigation. Ability to pay was therefore the key factor. Almost entirely overlooked by the ICB and Borradaile in their excitement over lease collections, litigation, and powers of attorney was the fact that the Northern Pacific and Manitoba Railway had built a branch line between Belmont and Hartney during the summer of 1898. Grain elevators were located at the new villages of Dunrea and Ninette, and the Lewis settlers no longer had to face the expensive, longer haul to Killarney. After ten years on the land, they were well placed to share in the prosperity that came to the area with the new railway. The only comment Borradaile made on the railway was to point out to the ICB that it had "greatly enhanced" the value of its lands. In fact, it was the combination of agricultural price increases, the new railway, and litigation that enabled Borradaile to collect lease installments — not litigation alone.

In the summer of 1902, an official of the Department of the Interior was asked to report on all crofter colonies in the Canadian West. At Pelican Lake, he noted a number of abandoned or sold properties and said that three families had moved to Saltcoats. Of those remaining on the land, he reported:

> These people are good farmers, they cultivate their land and
> do their work well. They are in a very thrifty condition and
> prospering, having overcome all their early troubles, and are in
> a fair way for progress.

The only grievance he encountered — one that was forcefully expressed by many — was the resentment over costs arising from legal actions brought by the ICB's solicitors, Tupper, Phippen and Tupper of Winnipeg, who were said by all to be "anxious for litigation."[10]

Equally anxious were the external creditors. After their refusal to accept the terms offered by the Scottish Office as recommended by Professor Rankine in 1897, the creditors were left to pursue their debtors on an individual basis. Donald MacLeod's property was assigned to a creditor in 1898, and over the next few years quit claims were registered against a dozen other properties. After 1897, the Scottish Office made no further attempt to facilitate the collection of the crofters' external debts.

THE CONCLUSION OF THE "EXPERIMENT"

At Saltcoats, the obvious inability to pay continued to win preferential treatment for the few remaining settlers. This did not extend to assisting the crofters to return to Scotland. A request for such assistance in 1895 from three family heads was not even considered by the ICB. Without exception, livestock and poultry by this time were registered in the names of family members not indebted to the ICB. This attempt to remove natural increase from the legal reach of the ICB's solicitors had become almost universal amongst the crofters at both Saltcoats and Pelican Lake by 1894, and was undoubtedly a response to Borradaile's initial legal opinion that the natural increase of the ICB's stock was ICB property. Interference in the management and sale of stock was thereby avoided, as was the possibility of legal claims by the ICB. By 1900, Borradaile's reports indicated that grain growing had been completely abandoned by all twelve settlers remaining in the Lothian Colony and that the only crop grown was potatoes. To the ICB's evident dismay, not one settler was willing to enter for a second homestead under the terms of the special legislation enacted for that purpose, all preferring to have eligible family members unencumbered by debt enter for new homesteads. Finally, in late 1900, the Scottish Office declared that no more concessions were to be extended and that the Saltcoats settlers were to be "treated with the extreme rigour of the law." The lease arrangements imposed at Pelican Lake in 1896 were to be imposed at Saltcoats in 1900. Scottish Office files unfortunately do not indicate whether the leases were signed or refused, but by May 1901 eviction notices had been issued and bailiffs involved. A letter to Clifford Sifton, from a sympathetic Saltcoats resident hurling the usual invective against Borradaile's "evil intentions," makes it clear that the process was not a pleasant one. Stewart Tupper and Borradaile combined to bring the full force of the law against the few remaining settlers. By September 1901, the ICB reported that seventy-one of its seventy-two Saltcoats properties had been abandoned. The statement reflected the legal position, not the actual one. Certificates of abandonment had been signed, but in the same report, Borradaile stated that eleven settlers were still on ICB-owned land.

If the ICB considered that the limits of its indulgence had been reached, by 1900 it shared with the Treasury an increasing concern over administrative expenditure. Each year seemed to require extraordinary costs beyond those for approved salaries and correspondence. In 1898, Statute Labour District No. 48 (Saltcoats) sued the Secretary for Scotland for defaulting on labour and fire taxes due on the abandoned properties. The costs of the local improvement taxes and school taxes in the Eden and Tupper school districts at Saltcoats amounted to $246.80 for the financial year ending 31 March 1900; the filling of wells and cellars on abandoned properties cost $330. The same bills amounted to $452.42 for the year ending 31 March 1903. The Canadian government insisted that the ICB was responsible for the seed-grain advances of 1890 and demanded payment of this long-overdue obligation. Inclusive of interest, over $1,100 was paid to the Department of the Interior by a reluctant ICB in October 1903. At Pelican Lake, the ICB's legal expenses could not all be charged against the settlers, and the more frequent visits by Borradaile increased incidental costs considerably.

The ICB, therefore, sought to extricate itself from its responsibility for its Canadian settlements. Initially, it was felt that the sale of abandoned lands at Saltcoats would recover practically the whole of the sums advanced to the settlers. However, the lands valued by Tupper at $3.50 an acre in 1893 could not be sold, even when Borradaile advertised them in 1899 at $2.00 per acre. As late as September 1901, not one of the ICB's quarter sections at Saltcoats had been sold. The ICB offered selected

Canadian mortgage companies the opportunity to take over its interests completely in April 1901, but all the companies responded that their business did not encompass such an undertaking. By early 1904, it was calculated that the process of collection at Pelican Lake would take five or six years, and that legal and administration expenses during that time could be as high as £3,000. Upon Colmer's recommendation, the ICB decided to offer a reduction of 20 percent to the Pelican Lake settlers upon condition that payment in full be received by 31 October 1904, and instructed Borradaile to seek a quick sale of the Saltcoats lands. In May 1904, the Under-Secretary for Scotland, summoned to appear before the Committee of Public Accounts, was able to agree that there was at last "a prospect of this tedious business coming to an end."

When it was learned that the Pelican Lake settlers were responding favourably to the ICB's offer, the Treasury grudgingly provided £75 for Colmer to visit Canada in December 1904 to wind up the affairs of the ICB. Colmer reported to the ICB upon his return that, with only two exceptions, all outstanding obligations at Pelican Lake had been paid, and that the ICB's lawyers had purchased the two remaining claims. The ICB no longer had obligations at Pelican Lake. At Saltcoats, sixteen properties, all in the former King Colony, had been sold at $3 per acre by 1903 and one young crofter had paid a portion of his debt. Colmer stated that three heads of families were in residence and that, though "considerable leniency" had been shown them due to their advanced ages, none had paid taxes or lease installments. The three were to be offered the opportunity to purchase their homesteads "at a moderate price" or face legal proceedings. Borradaile was dismissed as of 31 March 1905 and given a year's salary as a gratuity on Colmer's recommendation. The Royal Trust Company, at a yearly fee of £50 and a promise of a 5 percent sales commission, was made trustee of the remaining Saltcoats lands and instructed to sell them as soon as possible for a minimum price of $4 per acre. The ICB was determined not to sustain a loss on the "settlement experiment" and, with prices rising in the Saltcoats area, was confident that it would not do so. An offer from Stewart Tupper of $20,000 for the remaining Saltcoats lands in March 1906 was rejected as it would involve "paying too dearly for the opportunity of practically closing up the Board's work at once."

The ICB held its final meeting on 17 July 1906 and issued its *Fifteenth Report* in August. The document was largely self-congratulatory. An agreement had been signed by the Charles Sexton Company of Minneapolis to purchase all the remaining Saltcoats properties at $4 an acre. The Treasury would therefore receive more than the £13,120 in expenditures it had authorized since 1888. The Saltcoats settlers were said to have been "led away by bad advice" but were pronounced to be far better off in Canada than they would have been had they remained in Scotland. The Killarney settlements were judged to be "fairly successful," but the ICB added

> that the results might have been more satisfactory, both at Killarney and Saltcoats, had the Commission been given the opportunity of formulating its own scheme, and of personally selecting the families sent to Canada under its provisions.[11]

The principle of assisted emigration was thereby upheld while Lothian's scheme and the settlers themselves were found lacking in the essentials required.

The gloss alleged by the editor of the *Scottish Highlander* to have existed on the ICB's first report is clearly discernible on its last. No mention is made of the £8,584 spent in administration up to 31 March 1906. More significantly, statistical information is missing on the settlements themselves. The report did not state that of its fifty-six quarter sections near Pelican Lake, only forty-one original locations had passed to the assisted crofters or their successors, though as many as five others had been sold to other members of the families assisted by the ICB. At least nine properties belonged to people who had not come to Pelican Lake under the auspices of the ICB. Without a Canadian agent since Borradaile's dismissal, the ICB was probably unaware that a further eight properties changed hands almost immediately after the crofters gained title in 1903-04, some as a result of legal claims by T.J. Lawlor and other long-term creditors. Concerning the situation at Saltcoats, the final report is understandably reticent. Of the nearly one hundred individuals eligible to enter for homesteads near Saltcoats under ICB auspices, only seventy-two eventually did so, and by the date of the report, only two were in legal possession of the land.

However, the ICB's responsibilities did not end in 1906. In fact, the ICB was continued as "still engaged upon the business entrusted to them" upon George V's coronation in 1910 and was never to be officially disbanded. After 1906, the work of the ICB was entirely conducted through correspondence by Colmer and the Scottish Office. Decisions were required concerning unanticipated legal bills from Tupper, Phippen and Tupper and the unexpected full payment from one family head at Saltcoats in 1908. Archibald Ferguson thereby became the only family head at Saltcoats to gain title to the quarter section he was placed upon in 1889. Twice, the Charles Sexton Company asked for extensions of its installment dates as many of its settlers were failing to make their payments on time.

Both requests were firmly denied and on 1 November 1908, the Sexton Company made its final payment.

The Scottish Office, for years afterwards, considered whether to return the £2,000 in private subscriptions the original scheme had required in 1888. Finally, it was recognized that the names of most of the donors had gone unrecorded in the haste of collection in 1888 and 1889. On 13 January 1921, at Treasury insistence, Colmer paid the entire ICB bank balance of £3,262.18 into Treasury coffers. Ironically just a few months later, in response to the widespread unemployment following World War I, the British Parliament passed the *Empire Settlement Act*, authorizing a plan of emigration reminiscent of the long-forgotten Crofter and Cottar Colonisation Scheme of 1888. As a result, new reports by Poor Law officials on the prospects of emigration from Lewis and Harris soon were being examined at the Scottish Office.

For all its emphasis on finances, the ICB was not an impersonal bureaucracy, and the two men most concerned with its operation, therefore, deserve a final word. George Betts Borradaile, despite his strict concurrence with the ICB's paramount concern with finances, never gained the trust and respect of the Scottish Office. His reports were almost invariably received later than the Scottish Office thought appropriate, his accounting methods were consistently thought to be deficient, and his actions were often considered to have been taken without due authority. As the author of letters and reports that so often contained disappointing news, Borradaile perhaps inevitably suffered the common fate of the messenger conveying unwelcome information. On one occasion, Colmer referred to him as "Booradaile," and on another, a Scottish Office official facetiously suggested that, on the basis of his accounts, he should be thrown in prison.[12] At the same time, in the eyes of many crofter settlers Borradaile resembled no one so closely as the factor of a Highland estate. After a series of extended illnesses, Borradaile moved from Winnipeg to Medicine Hat in 1900 to take a second job with the Hudson's Bay Company, and from there conducted his administration of the settlements for the last five years of his employment by the ICB. He refused to assist the ICB in any way after 1906 and had to be asked by Colmer if he had ever received his gratuity. He rarely spoke of his sixteen years as Crofter Commissioner and died in 1908, having become a justice of the peace at Medicine Hat.

J.G. Colmer, on the other hand, was held in the highest regard by members of the ICB. The Secretary for Scotland in 1908 wrote that disaster had only been averted as a result of Colmer's skill and conduct. Colmer ended a career of twenty-three years at the Office of the High

Commission in 1903 to take up employment with a London financial firm. His salary as ICB secretary ended in 1905, but as late as 1927 he was still communicating with the Scottish Office in connection with ICB affairs. He yearned for a formal conclusion to the ICB's work, and for several years urged a meeting of the ICB to consider the *Sixteenth Report* he had prepared.[13] Though the Scottish Office occasionally considered recommending him for an honour in connection with his work as ICB secretary, records indicate he received only a brief letter of appreciation from the Under-Secretary for Scotland in 1926.

CHAPTER SIX

The Historical Consequences
of "Emigration Roulette"

Considering the significance of the work of the ICB, the absence of an assessment of it in the histories of both Scotland and Canada is surprising. From the Scottish viewpoint, the fact that the ICB administered settlements located in Canada may account in part for this lack of attention. Yet the settlement scheme was formulated to address one of the most intractable and long-standing issues in the entire modern history of Scotland. From the Canadian viewpoint, the settlements were small, were established prior to the flood of immigration that occurred later, and have not been perceived as having influenced the course of Canadian immigration history. But, on both sides of the Atlantic, Lothian's scheme had an immediate and profound influence on public policy that has yet to be acknowledged.

Lord Lothian indicated no interest in the widespread national debate on state-aided emigration in the 1880s. He was not a member of Lord Brabazon's National Association for Promoting State-Directed Emigration and Colonization and made no attempt to link his proposals for crofter emigration to the wider agitation. His settlement scheme was endorsed in April 1888 by a Cabinet which expected daily to receive a mature proposal from the National Association and which was aware that 160 MPs and Lords supported the Association's objectives. Historians have failed to explore the connection between the National Association lobby and the surprising endorsement Lothian's scheme received from Cabinet. Even if the Scottish and the national schemes were unrelated in origin and in politics, their destinies were bound by the Select Committee proposed by W.H. Smith on 22 November 1888 to examine crofter settlement schemes. By the time it was appointed in April 1889, the Committee's mandate had grown to include all assisted emigration schemes. But the bulk of the testimony it received concerned the crofters settled in the Canadian West under Lothian's scheme because that was the only substantial scheme then under trial. Ostensibly reporting on the principles of assisted emigration, the *Report of the Colonisation Committee* dealt primarily with the practice and prospects of assisted emigration from the Scottish Highlands. The difficulties experienced at Pelican Lake and especially at Saltcoats were so thoroughly examined that the proponents of state-aided emigration were consistently on the defensive. The report finally issued in 1891 contained only a tepid endorsement of Lothian's scheme, and its general tone was a considerable discouragement to the emigrationists.[1] The consequent withering of the lobby for state aid for emigration was due at least as much to the specific experience of the Canadian settlements as it was to the improvement in the British economy. George Trevelyan had no difficulty in 1893 in announcing the absolute termination of consideration of state aid for all colonization schemes using the crofter experiment in Canada as his sole justification.

Lothian, in contrast to Trevelyan, was encouraged by the Committee's meek endorsement and took the opportunity to make a rare speech on his scheme in the House of Lords. With a fresh parliamentary vote of £7,500, he sought to reactivate the channels and processes of 1888 and 1889. The Edinburgh Board of Supervision, however, refused to allow Malcolm McNeill or any other of its officers to impair their influence through the implication of a "direct connection with the scheme." It is indicative of how heavily Lothian depended upon McNeill that no alternate "selector" was contemplated before Lothian relinquished office in October 1892. His successor, Sir George Trevelyan, found that Lothian's circular of 1892 had failed to elicit a single application from the parishes from which the Saltcoats and Pelican Lake settlers had been drawn. Rejecting all applications from elsewhere in the Highlands and Islands on the grounds that the scheme had been conceived to apply only to the Western Isles, Trevelyan insisted that the proposed 1893 emigration should not take place.

Ironically, nothing more clearly demonstrates the absolute correctness of the thinking behind the McNeill-Lothian scheme than the complete absence of applications from Lewis and Harris during the winter of 1892-93. In 1888-89, with the initially favourable reports from the Pelican Lake settlers, a widespread interest in the government scheme was expressed throughout the Western Isles despite a concerted Land League opposition. The number of families that emigrated in April 1889 was nearly the maximum possible under the scheme for that year. The disappearance of that interest has been variously attributed to the escalation of Land League activity, improving economic conditions in the Islands, increased employment opportunities due to government projects, the work of the Crofters Commission, and the traditional disinclination of crofters to emigrate. While the influence of all these factors must be acknowledged, it is necessary to state that they were all as operative in 1889 as in 1892. The one new factor, and thus a key discouragement to government-assisted emigration in 1892, was the existence of persistent public and private reports of the trials and disappointments of the emigrants of 1888 and 1889. The precise opposite of the inducement envisioned by McNeill and Lothian had been created.

The role of the Canadian government in the settlement scheme was, from the very beginning, confused and marred by inefficiency. The inability of the Department of the Interior to provide land for homestead locations in 1888 was largely a consequence of the hasty implementation of the scheme. Other difficulties encountered were attributable to the same cause, but problems were compounded by the persistent inefficiency of the Canadian government. For example, the formal British request for cooperation in April 1888 asked the Canadian government to act immediately to appoint a member to the ICB and to grant the ICB full legal powers under Canadian law. Only after much prodding by the Colonial Office did the Canadian Privy Council agree in October to Tupper's appointment; it then neglected to inform British authorities of its decision. The legislation requested was passed in May 1888, but was immediately found to be inadequate. Once the settlements were established, the only legislation requested of the Canadian government was that sought by the ICB in 1895 to enable the Saltcoats settlers to select second homesteads under ICB auspices. The amendment to the *Dominion Lands Act* was not enacted until eighteen months after it had been agreed to, and even then, the Department of the Interior did not act under its altered provisions. The Liberal administration in Canada seemed as confused by the scheme as its Conservative predecessor.

Despite the formal involvement of the Canadian government, despite the numerous visitations of Canadian dignitaries to the colonies, and despite the active participation of Dominion Lands officials in 1889, the Canadian authorities were curiously content to leave the scheme's administration in British hands. The refusal to commit Canadian government funds to the experiment and the undignified severance of the Department of the Interior from its active involvement with the Saltcoats settlement in 1889 have already been referred to.[2] The desire to disassociate from the "Imperial experiment" was so strong that Tupper was forced to enquire if withdrawal of Canadian participation was contemplated. On more than one occasion, he had to lecture the Minister of the Interior on the wider implications of the colonization scheme for Western settlement. The lesson was apparently still unlearned by the Department of Agriculture as late as 1890. John Lowe, the Deputy Minister, had stated in 1888 that the "whole effort" of the Department was to bring out immigrants to people the Canadian West. Yet, when questioned two years later by the Canadian Select

Committee on Agriculture and Colonization on the reports of destitution in the crofter settlements, Lowe was clearly surprised at the line of questioning, stating that the scheme was "not in any way aided or particularly invited by the Department. It is purely an Imperial tentative effort."[3] When the Committee pointed out that British Columbia's effort to attract crofter immigration could be jeopardized by reports of destitution, Lowe undertook to launch an investigation. It is apparent that, while the Scottish Office was fully aware of the implications of such reports upon its proclaimed policies, Canadian authorities (with the notable exception of the Office of the High Commission in London) were remarkably naive about the effect the failure of the crofter settlements could have upon the prospects of Canada's policies in the West.

This naivety diminished as negative reports of the Saltcoats settlement continued to receive wide publicity and as emigration from the north of Scotland fell far below normal expectations. In 1892, Lowe stated before the Canadian Select Committee on Agriculture and Colonization:

> The immigration market is exceedingly sensitive, and the least thing in the shape of bad reports will incite a very important drawback. One bad report will do a great deal more harm than fifty good reports will do.[4]

In 1892, the highly parsimonious Department of the Interior appointed an emigration agent in Inverness, against the opinion of Sir Charles Tupper that the additional expense was unjustified. Especially until 1895, the agent reported a widespread interest in the crofter settlements and a strong aversion in the crofting parishes to further emigration to Canada. Though improving economic conditions and the raised expectations created by Liberal Highland Commissions are credited with severely depressing the numbers of prospective emigrants, Canadian authorities after 1892 acknowledged that the burden of responsibility for the public perception of Canada in Britain rested with Canadians, even with regard to an "Imperial tentative effort" at colonization on Canadian soil.

Of the Canadian authorities, only the Office of the Canadian High Commission clearly and consistently understood the implications of Lothian's scheme for Western settlement. Sir Charles Tupper and Colmer repeatedly impressed upon the departments of Agriculture and the Interior the need to look beyond the immediate settlement problems to the broader Canadian interest in encouraging immigration. Until 1892, the success of the settlements was sought to permit the further expenditure of Imperial funds; after 1892, that same success was required to encourage private emigration. With the change of government in the United Kingdom in 1892, the new British authorities argued that difficulties experienced in the Canadian settlements were attributable to inherent weakness in the Conservative scheme. The High Commission had no such easy explanation. It urged recognition of the hardships imposed upon the settlers by adverse economic and climatic factors, but could only press such an argument to a limited extent without injuring the prospects of the very emigration it sought to encourage. The disappointing results, especially at Saltcoats, were therefore predictably attributed to the class of settlers involved — the crofters themselves.

This explanation was forcefully proffered at the same time the ICB was seeking applications for the proposed 1893 emigration. Though it accorded perfectly with long-held prejudices of Scottish Office officials, it produced the sharpest division of opinion that was ever to occur amongst the scheme's administrators. Malcolm McNeill angrily rejected Colmer's assertion that the Saltcoats settlers were inferior to the Pelican Lake settlers. He attributed the problems at Saltcoats to the "gross and shameful apathy of the Canadians" in failing to select and prepare land as promised. The Under-Secretary reminded Trevelyan that it was time the settlers looked to Canada for help and later authorized the seed-grain advance of 1893 only because he agreed with McNeill that "the Canadian government did not act fairly to these people." The Scottish Office insisted on removing from the draft of the *Fourth Report* prepared by Colmer the strongly worded statement on the inferiority of the Saltcoats settlers. When the exchange culminated in Trevelyan's denunciation of the scheme and its settlers during Tupper's investigation of the Saltcoats complaints in September 1893, both Tupper and Colmer would have been fully aware that Canada's reputation as a field for settlement had received a calculated and serious setback.

The reputation of the Scots as settlers also experienced a serious, if temporary, reversal. When a parliamentary member of Britain's Emigrants Information Office visited Killarney in 1894, he found a local community which "could not say anything too bad" of the crofters, regarding them as poor workers and "thoroughly bad farmers." This is not to suggest that this bitter opinion was anything more than a local phenomenon. Yet, in 1895, when the return of the Conservatives to power in Britain led to renewed interest in the British Columbia crofter settlement scheme, the Canadian Minister of the Interior was informed by the British Columbia government that it had no intention of encouraging "such a class of settlers" to come to British Columbia. Alexander Begg, British Columbia's "crofter commissioner" from 1888 to 1891, received no official encouragement in his attempts to revive the scheme in 1896.[5] For the first time in Canadian history, Highland Scots had become classed with such "undesirable" groups as the Irish and East End Londoners. While the British Columbia opinion derived partially from local politics, the reputation of the prairie settlements had certainly contributed to this view.

More speculatively, it may be stated that, as a comparatively large and well-publicized scheme, the reputation of the crofter settlements contributed to the growing opinion that the British did not make good settlers. The Barr colonists were certainly not the first British group to receive widespread publicity for their agricultural shortcomings; the crofters gained that reputation more than a decade earlier.[6] Though many smaller groups of British settlers abandoned homesteads in the 1880s and 1890s, those settled under Lothian's scheme were more numerous and their problems more publicized. Moreover, their reputation cannot have escaped the notice of Clifford Sifton, who was a provincial Cabinet minister in Manitoba before becoming Laurier's Minister of the Interior in 1897. The crofter settlements near Pelican Lake were in the provincial constituency adjacent to his own and, as Manitoba's Attorney-General, Sifton would have been aware of the many legal actions brought by local implement dealers against the crofters there. As a member of Thomas Greenway's Cabinet, he was familiar with Manitoba's concerns over the crofters becoming public charges in 1895 and with the decisions to finance the delegations to London in 1896 and 1897. When he took over as Minister of the Interior early in 1897, Sifton instituted sweeping changes in personnel, organization, and policy. Henry Hall Smith at Winnipeg and Thomas Grahame at Glasgow lost their positions in the departmental reorganization. Sifton's settlement policies changed the face of western Canada. His aversion to assisted settlements as well as his preference for non-British settlers are both highly suggestive that the difficulties of the crofter settlements were well known to him. Organized British settlement would never again be expected to play a significant role in the Canadian West.

Of course, such weighty historical concerns were the last topics to occupy the minds of the seventy-nine families as they left Scotland. Their first concern was to continue a way of life that they recognized was seriously threatened by harsh economic realities and by population pressures in the Islands themselves. The idea of overseas colonies had combined with poverty, necessity, and hope to produce the decision to emigrate. However, the decision was tentatively taken and was wholeheartedly embraced by few, if any, of the emigrants. Were they, as many of their neighbours suggested, simply the first victims of another clearance, the dupes of a government serving landlords intent on weakening the cause of Highland land reform? Nothing more clearly demonstrates the strength of these doubts than the vacillation and last-minute refusal to depart of so many of the originally selected individuals and families.

There can be no doubt that the emigration scheme was designed to serve landed interests. It was avowedly an alternative to radical land reform proposals. Neither is it simply coincidental that the scheme was put forward at a time when the local population was vulnerable due to diminishing incomes and food supplies. But the manner of the emigrants' selection and departure provides no support for the view that they were victims of coercive policies comparable to those applied by James Matheson on Lewis in the 1850s or by the Duke of Sutherland earlier in the century.[7] Though their frequent petitions indicated that a number of the colonists continued to view themselves as victims, neither government nor ICB policies actually discriminated against the crofter settlers. The crofters correctly sensed that they were pawns in the public policies of both Scotland and Canada, but it cannot be said that they were the victims of those public policies.[8]

If the emigrants sought a continuation of their Highland way of life, the Canadian West in the late nineteenth century did not prove as conducive to that purpose as the maritime provinces had in the late eighteenth century. The traditional combination of agricultural pursuits with externally earned cash wages was continued, but the demands of commercial agriculture and the necessity of debt repayment required a rapid change in cultural norms. Yet the most persistent theme in Borradaile's reports to the ICB is his criticism of the settlers' agricultural methods. Even when reporting on the bumper crop of 1901, he complained that production would be higher if the settlers would not "insist on sowing the same seed year after year." Nonetheless, prosperity was such that nearly all remaining settlers near Pelican Lake were able to discharge their obligations to the ICB and gain title to their properties between 1901 and 1905. At Saltcoats, a Canadian government agent reported in 1902 that younger family members were adapting much more readily to the ways of the country than their "too conservative" parents. The persistence of a substantial crofter colony prior to World War I to the north of the original ICB locations near Saltcoats suggests more "success" than the ICB acknowledged, and it is significant that this colony attracted some of the Pelican Lake crofters. Lord Lothian's scheme, therefore, did ultimately succeed in establishing crofter colonies in the Canadian West; but, the fiasco at Saltcoats destroyed any illusions he may have had that Canadian settlements could resolve questions of Scottish politics. The Scottish Office remained perplexed at the sharply contrasting fates of the Canadian settlements, and in 1905 Colmer frankly stated that he could not account for the differences. The settlements at Saltcoats and Pelican Lake were both entirely comprised of the same small crofter and cottar classes. Why then, were their fates so different?

The colonists had all arrived suffering the same disadvantages more or less equally. Hurriedly selected and dispatched, there had been no time to augment their meager cash resources through the sale of Scottish possessions. For the Lewis emigrants of 1888, the sum initially available to each family head was substantially diminished by local debt payments before they had even left the Western Isles. For the Argyle and Saltcoats settlers, large family size resulted in the high travel costs that so seriously alarmed those charged with settling the crofters in Canada. Scarth was adamant that £100 was the minimum required for settlement and farm-establishment purposes after arrival at the Canadian destination.[9] He regarded the £60 to £70 actually available to most family heads as grossly inadequate. At Pelican Lake, the additional funds secured by Scarth, when added to the advances for provisions and seed grain, were some-what more substantial than the funds subsequently made available at Saltcoats, where the crofters paid for their first year's rations out of their original advances. Assuming the costs of farm-making to have been com-parable at Saltcoats and Pelican Lake, the advantage gained by the Pelican Lake settlers was perhaps significant, but not substantial enough to account for the colonies' differing fortunes.

Essentially, the game of "emigration roulette" initiated by Lothian at the Scottish Office gave three advantages to the Killarney and Argyle set-tlers and none to the Saltcoats settlers. The lands around Pelican Lake upon which the 1888 immigrants were located were well-suited for the production of cereal crops. Situated amongst established farmers, the 1888 crofter groups had extensive, if fluctuating, local wage-earning op-portunities available to them. In the early years of the colony's life, the local merchant community at Killarney did not hesitate to extend credit to the settlers in the belief that both Canadian and Imperial authorities had undertaken responsibility for all debts. In short, the material advan-tages of the Pelican Lake crofters were immense when compared with the situation of the Saltcoats settlers who were located upon land of questionable quality, were competing for scarce local employment in an undeveloped economy, and were denied credit with local merchants by order of the ICB. The two settlements faced the years of adverse eco-nomic and climatic conditions following their establishment from dramatically different perspectives.

If the reasons for the failure of the settlement scheme were clearly inher-ent in the scheme itself, questions raised during this examination of the scheme strike at the heart of the traditional view of the role of the Scot in Canadian history. There is no evidence here to suggest that Scottish birth brought an easy success or facilitated the adaptation to Canadian circumstances. In fact, the evidence strongly suggests that the attitudes and practices brought from the Western Isles distinctly inhibited that adaptation. So, too, did the conservatism with which the settlers clung to the social and political traditions of the Highlands. Their agricultural methods were disparaged by a number of observers. The tendency to remain socially distinct from other settlers and to seek redress from Scotland of their many grievances contributed to the difficulties of adaptation. The extreme lengths to which the Canadian government went to avoid responsibility for them indicates that Canada offered no special considerations to these settlers based upon their ethnicity. The lingering impression is that Canada was simply a reluctant host to uncertain settlers.

The problems encountered by the seventy-nine families of Highland immigrants had a profound effect upon the policies of both the British and Canadian governments. Not until after World War I could a British government again contemplate state involvement in emigration. Under the auspices of the Empire Settlement Scheme, the British settlers who arrived in the Canadian West in the 1920s entered a society in which the ethnic makeup had changed dramatically over the previous thirty years. The altered circumstances were the direct result of the major shift in Canadian policy and opinion concerning British agriculturalists that occurred at the end of the nineteenth century. The prairie experience of the crofter families selected under Lothian's scheme of emigration and settlement contributed materially to that change.

As for the settlers themselves, within a few years Canada became their new home. Very few ever returned to Scotland, though the Islands were never far from their thoughts. Their Canadian neighbours understood neither the Scottish politics nor the settlement scheme that brought the crofters to the West, and continued to view them as "favoured"; modern prairie farmers have more understanding of debt loads and repayment schedules. Today, the descendants of the crofters live primarily in Ontario, western Canada, and the northern United States, their North American destinies shaped irrevocably by men whose names are largely forgotten: Colmer, Scarth, Borradaile, McNeill, Tupper, Lothian. As Canadian tourists, many now travel to see the Western Isles of Scotland, the leaving of which caused such great distress to their grandparents, the crofters.

Epilogues

As INDICATED earlier, the response of the British Empire to the crofters' dilemma in the Western Isles was substantial. Malcolm McNeill was concerned that seed potatoes being distributed on Lewis while he was first advertising for families to emigrate to Canada might convince the people that there was no need to leave. The money to purchase the potatoes had been raised in Queensland. At one time or another, settlement proposals were received at the Scottish Office from New Zealand, British Columbia, Tasmania, and Natal.

The legislation passed by New Zealand in 1884 setting aside a reserve on the North Island for crofter-fisherman certainly appealed initially to the Scottish Office. However, the expensive passage rates and the absence of legislation comparable to Canada's *Dominion Lands Act* made the scheme less attractive. Similar considerations prevented Scottish officials from pursuing a Tasmanian proposal that crofters provide the labour force to develop the deep-sea fishery for the growing Australian market.

One proposal that did receive the support of the Scottish Office was that received from British Columbia, also aimed at developing a deep-sea fishery with crofter labour. An arrangement was tentatively reached in late 1887 that would have seen the Imperial government loan £150,000 to British Columbia for crofter colonization. Disagreement over financial details caused the scheme to be postponed until after the Select Committee on Colonisation reported in 1891. British Columbia then hesitated for over a year before Premier Robson travelled to London to make final arrangements. Robson's unexpected death in London, and the discouraging reports from the prairie crofter colonies, dampened the province's enthusiasm. As a result, this "gigantic scheme" was never implemented.

The British Columbia proposal had been motivated in part by the desire to replace "undesirable and unreliable" Chinese and Indian labour in its coastal fishery. A similar motivation resulted in the most bizarre and most expensive proposal of them all. From Natal, the Scottish Office received details of a scheme to replace black labour in the South African gold fields with crofters indentured for a term of five years. At the end of the five years, each crofter would receive a 6,000-acre farm, £25,000 in cash, and cows "all within a wire fence." The anticipated cost of the proposal was to be nearly £5 million. The files at the Scottish Record Office contain no record of what must have been a very brief official response to this proposal.

* * *

History, as the common adage insists, has a way of repeating itself. In 1907, Lady Gordon Cathcart, whose assisted emigration of a few families in 1883 and 1884 caused such hope in the hearts of Malcolm McNeill and Lord Lothian, again sought ways to extricate herself from difficulties on her island estates. She requested photographs from the Department of the Interior of established crofters in the Canadian West. Her aim was the same as it had been a quarter of a century earlier — to encourage some of her tenants to move to Canada. Ironically, the photographs she received were not of her own Wapella settlements; nor were they of the established crofter communities near Pelican Lake. Lady Cathcart received from Canadian officials four photographs of crofter homesteads near Saltcoats in the new province of Saskatchewan.

* * *

The controversies surrounding the Saltcoats properties did not end with their sale to the Charles Sexton Company. As a result of agitation by the *Yorkton Enterprise* in 1911, the Department of the Interior attempted to enforce provisions of Section 44 of the *Dominion Lands Act* requiring *bona fide* settlers to be placed on lands held by colonization companies. The *Enterprise* argued that the still vacant quarter sections, formerly assigned to the crofters, should be thrown open for homesteading and the ICB and its American successors were accordingly sued by the Department of the Interior. This "cloud on the title" — an ironically appropriate legal metaphor if ever there was one — resulted in complicated litigation that was not cleared up until after World War I.

In preparation for the legal actions, valuations of the properties were required and, in October 1910, a Homestead Inspector, accompanied by Charles Docherty and Archibald Ferguson, examined the quarter sections selected by the forty-nine families during the chaotic summer of 1889. The emotions of Docherty and Ferguson were not recorded, but on many of the valuation reports the inspector noted that much of the land had returned to prairie and wrote, "There is evidence of old buildings having been on this land as well as old breaking having been done some time ago." The statement could stand as a fitting epitaph to the hopes of the settlers and to the work of the ICB.

* * *

While Malcolm McNeill regretted the haste with which his plans were implemented, he consistently blamed the scheme's failure on the "gross and shameful apathy of the Canadians" in failing to select and prepare land as promised. In 1906, when the ICB issued its final report, boasting that all moneys advanced had been recovered due to land sales and repayments from the emigrant crofters and their descendants, McNeill wrote to *The Scotsman* outlining the "outrage" surrounding the broken promises made to the 1889 emigrants by the Canadians. In the same letter, he absolved Lothian of any responsibility. As surprising as the Canadian negligence was, it was but one more consequence of the destructive haste with which Lothian implemented the scheme so long held dear by Malcolm McNeill. How completely the well-considered scheme sought by McNeill might have succeeded will never be known. The fiasco launched by Lothian in 1888 ensured that it could never be attempted.

* * *

At one time or another, three of the major players in the settlement scheme sought the appointment of Crofter Commissioner.

W.B. Scarth was tired of his political responsibilities and advised Prime Minister Macdonald that his life in Winnipeg had become "a burden." In September and October of 1888, he urged both Tupper and Macdonald to press for his appointment as managing trustee of the crofter settlements. The fact that he expected a salary equivalent to the income and benefits he received as MP for Winnipeg probably explains why nothing more was heard of the proposal.

Colin Macleay, the Saltcoats schoolteacher, was a more unlikely applicant. Accompanying the petition of the Saltcoats crofters that he forwarded to the Scottish Office in May 1893 was a letter addressed to Sir George Trevelyan, the Scottish Secretary. In the letter, Macleay brought allegations of incompetence and dishonesty against Borradaile and urged that he be replaced. At the same time, Macleay contacted a number of people in Scotland, stating that the appointment of Crofter Commissioner should more appropriately be his. The campaign resulted in a Scottish MP officially urging his appointment upon the Scottish Office. An article published in July 1893 by the *Scottish Highlander* about the problems at Saltcoats was also a result of Macleay's correspondence. Although the ICB was certainly dissatisfied with Borradaile at the time, it would not even consider replacing him with so single-minded an advocate of the crofters as Colin Macleay. Tupper saw Macleay as the cause of the difficulties at Saltcoats, not as an agent who might help to resolve them.

Henry Hall Smith was one of the casualties when Clifford Sifton decided to shake up the Department of the Interior. Suddenly unemployed, he drew to the attention of the Scottish Office his familiarity with the crofters due to his involvement in their settlement process and to his subsequent work as a voluntary member of the Winnipeg subcommittee.

He offered his services to the ICB in May 1897. The offer was politely declined.

* * *

The thirteen settlers whose liens were retained by the CNWL after the dust had settled in 1893 were never referred to again in ICB or Scottish Office records. Yet they were subject to the same hopes and disappointments as the ICB settlers. In the Argyle colony, the CNWL properties comprised nearly half the crofter settlement. It might be expected that their successes and failures would be comparable to their relatives under ICB sponsorship. In fact, their success rate was much lower. The CNWL did not offer its settlers the lease extensions granted by the ICB in 1897, and expected its settlers to repay their debts by the turn of the century as scheduled. In addition, the land company applied its standard 8 percent interest rate rather than the ICB's rate of just over 4 percent. Whereas twelve of the ICB's fifteen settlers in the Argyle colony gained title to their homesteads, only six of the CNWL's settlers did the same.

One of the disappointed settlers was Kenneth MacMillan, aged twenty-seven when he arrived at Hilton with the Bannatyne Mackinnon party. Though the statement about "sending gold home soon" was not his, MacMillan did share in the optimism that prevailed in the Argyle colony. He wrote a very favourable letter to the *Glasgow Herald* in the autumn of 1888. Within a short time, he had married Mackinnon's daughter and set to work to pay his debt of just over $300 to the CNWL. But by the summer of 1893 Kenneth MacMillan was dead, and the land company was obliged to pay the property's municipal taxes. The location of Kenneth MacMillan's grave is unrecorded.

* * *

Many dreams died at Pelican Lake and Saltcoats as a result of the "tentative effort" at colonization begun in 1888. The hopes of policy makers were dashed and the grief experienced by the settlers can barely be imagined by us one hundred years later.

But many dreams were also born. The descendants of the original settlers are scattered now from coast to coast, though many still reside in the Pelican Lake area. In July 1988, two separate reunions occurred there. At Hilton, the descendants of the Harris emigrants gathered on 1-3 July. They heard a sermon in Gaelic and saw Murray McKay, a direct descendant of one of the original crofter settlers, receive a centennial farm sign and certificate from the Manitoba government. On 18-19 July, more than 200 descendants of the Lewis settlers gathered at Ninette. An exhibition by the J.A.V. David Museum at Killarney was presented, and Sandy

Macdonald received a centennial plaque celebrating one hundred years of residence by his family on the original homestead.

* * *

In 1888, Mary Stewart, aged twenty-one, agreed to accompany the Allan MacLeod party to Manitoba. At the last moment, she hesitated and remained in Lewis. She married Murdo McSween and the young couple were among the forty-nine families who left the Western Isles in 1889 for Saltcoats. McSween was one of those sent by Borradaile from the King Colony to work at Rat Portage. He became ill, and died at Winnipeg in November 1890. Mary McSween, widowed and bitterly disappointed with her Canadian experience, was determined to return to Scotland with her nine-month-old child. Again she hesitated. Deciding finally to stay in Canada, Mary McSween went to relatives near Killarney and never saw the island of Lewis again. In 1988, at the centennial reunion, her granddaughter said:

> Thank God for the determination, stubbornness, courage and ingenuity that he had bestowed on her, which leaves us, her descendants, here in this great land of ours today.

Appendices

Appendix I-a				
ICB Lands Near Pelican Lake: The Killarney Colony[1]				
Admin. No.	Name of Settler	Location (W1)	Disposition of Land
1	William MacLeod	NE 3.5.17	to settler 1904
34	Malcolm McIver	NE 33.4.17	to non-crofter 1904
2	Donald MacDonald	NE 9.5.17	to settler 1905
54	Samuel Graham	NW 5.5.17	to settler 1903
4	John Mackay	SE 35.4.17	to settler 1905
5	Norman Graham	NE 21.4.17	to non-crofter 1904
35	William MacLeod	NW 17.5.17	to settler 1903
6	John Nicolson	SW 25.4.17	to settler 1905
36	John McLean	SE 25.4.17	to settler 1903
56	Murdo MacLeod	NE 25.4.17	to settler 1900
7	John Campbell	SW 13.5.17	to settler 1904
37	Angus Graham	NW 31.4.16	to Saltcoats crofter 1905
8	John Mackenzie Jr.	SW 27.4.17	to settler 1905
38	Andrew Graham	NE 1.5.17	to settler 1893
9	John MacLeod	SE 23.4.17	to "unassisted crofter" 1905
39	William MacLeod	NW 23.4.17	to non-crofter 1900
40	John MacLeod Jr.	SW 23.4.17	to non-crofter 1900
57	Lewis MacLeod	SW 3.5.17	to "unassisted crofter" 1899
10	Kenneth Macauley	SE 33.4.17	to settler 1902
53	John Macauley	NW 33.4.17	to settler 1905
73	Neil Munro	NE 5.5.17	to settler 1903
11	Angus MacDonald	SW 9.5.17	to settler 1905
58	John Mackenzie	SW 35.4.17	to settler 1903
13	Angus MacLeod	NW 25.4.17	to other crofter 1905
41	Donald MacLeod	NE 23.4.17	to creditor 1898
14	John Morrison	SE 9.5.17	to settler 1905
59	Murdo Morrison	SE 17.5.17	to widow 1908
15	John Graham	SW 31.4.16	to settler 1905
60	John Graham (cousin of #15)	NE 17.5.17	to settler 1903
16	Allan MacLeod	NW 9.5.17	to settler 1905
42	Murdo Stewart	SE 5.5.17	to settler 1905
17	John Mackenzie Sr.	SE 27.4.17	to settler 1905
43	Colin Mackenzie	NE 27.4.17	to grandson 1903
61	Kenneth MacLeod	SW 5.5.17	to other crofter 1903
18	William Macdonald	NE 31.4.16	to settler 1903
55	Alexander Macdonald	SE 31.4.16	to other crofter 1903
44	Donald Murray	SW 17.15.17	to settler 1904
19	Murdo Graham	NW 13.5.17	to settler 1903
21	Norman Mackenzie	SE 21.4.17	to widow 1908
45	William Mackenzie	NW 21.4.17	to settler 1905
62	James McIver	SW 21.4.17	to Saltcoats crofter 1903
63	Malcolm Mackenzie	NW 19.4.16	to CNWL 1893

Admin. No.	Name of Settler	Location (W1)	Disposition of Land
	Appendix I-b		
	ICB Lands Near Pelican Lake: The Argyle Colony		
22	John MacDonald Jr.	NW 21.5.16	to widow 1909
46	Norman MacDonald	SW 21.5.16	to settler 1900
64	Duncan MacDonald	NW 7.5.15	to settler 1902
23	John MacDonald Sr.	NE 17.5.16	to settler 1903
47	William MacDonald	SE 21.5.16	to CNWL 1893
24	Angus MacLeod	SE 21.5.16	to settler 1902
65	Alex Morrison	NW 27.6.16	to CNWL 1893
25	Angus Morrison	NW 15.6.16	abandoned
66	Archibald Morrison	NE 9.6.16	to CNWL 1893
26	Donald Mackinnon[2]	SW 21.6.16	to settler 1903
48	Kenneth Mackinnon	NW 33.6.16	to CNWL 1893
67	Catherine Mackinnon	NE 17.6.16	to settler 1903
27	Donald Stewart	NE 15.6.16	to son 1903
49	Kenneth Stewart	SW 13.6.16	to CNWL 1893
68	William MacLeod	SW 15.6.16	to CNWL 1893
28	Ronald Mackay	NE 23.6.16	to non-crofter 1903
29	Dugald Mackenzie	NW 21.6.16	to son 1902
69	Donald Mackenzie	NE 21.6.16	to CNWL 1893
70	John McKay	NE 19.6.16	to CNWL 1893
71	Hugh Morrison	NW 19.6.16	to CNWL 1893
30	Roderick Mackay	SE 23.6.16	to son 1905
72	John Mackay	NE 13.6.16	to CNWL 1893
31	Bannatyne Mackinnon	NW 23.6.16	to settler 1903
50	Kenneth MacMillan	SW 23.6.16	to CNWL 1893
32	Kenneth MacLeod	NW 13.6.16	to settler 1905
33	John Fraser	NE 7.5.15	to non-crofter 1904
51	Donald Fraser	SE 7.5.15	to CNWL 1894

Sources: SRO, AF 51 files; Reports of the Imperial Colonisation Board; CNWL Co. files; Manitoba Land Titles Office records.

Appendix II-a			
ICB Lands Near Saltcoats: The Lothian Colony			
Admin. No.	Name of Settler	Location (W2)	Disposition of Land
2	Kenneth McIver	SE 10.25.1	to Sexton 1906
51	Murdo McIver	SW 10.25.1	to Sexton 1906
5	Malcolm McKay	SW 10.25.2	to Sexton 1906
54	Donald McKay	SE 10.25.2	to Sexton 1906
95	Neil McKay	NE 14.25.2	to Sexton 1906
6	Donald Morrison	SW 27.25.2	to Sexton 1906
7	Norman Macauley	NE 3.25.1	to Sexton 1906
10	Donald MacDonald	Left before located	
11	Charles Docherty	SW 16.25.1	to Sexton 1906
58	John Docherty	SE 16.25.1	to Sexton 1906
12	Alexander MacDonald	NW 9.25.1	to Sexton 1906
13	Malcolm McLeod	NW 34.24.2	to Sexton 1906
14	Donald Graham	NW 2.25.1	to Sexton 1906
15	Angus Smith	SE 4.25.2	to Sexton 1906
60	Roderick Smith	NE 4.25.2	to Sexton 1906
16	Alexander McLean	NE 32.24.2	to Sexton 1906
61	Alexander McLean	NW 32.24.2	to Sexton 1906
17	John McLean	SE 32.24.2	to Sexton 1906
62	Angus McLean	SW 32.24.2	to Sexton 1906
63	John McLeod	NW 28.24.2	to Sexton 1906
18	Duncan McLeod	SW 19.25.1	to Sexton 1906
64	Murdo McLeod	NE 18.25.1	to Sexton 1906
19	Donald McKay	NW 33.25.1	to Sexton 1906
65	Norman McKay	SE 24.25.2	to Sexton 1906
20	Allan Kenneth Murray	SW 34.25.2	to Sexton 1906
21	Finlay McLean	NW 32.25.1	to Sexton 1906
22	Alexander Mitchell	SW 1.25.1	to Sexton 1906
68	Neil McLeod	NE 1.25.1	to Sexton 1906
23	Donald McLeod	NW 19.25.1	to Sexton 1906
24	Malcolm McDonald	NW 17.25.1	to Sexton 1906
25	Donald MacDonald	SE 17.25.1	to Sexton 1906
71	Murdo MacDonald	SE 18.25.1	to Sexton 1906
26	Angus Mackay	NE 32.25.1	to Sexton 1906
27	Malcolm McLeod	NE 2.25.1	to Sexton 1906
28	Robert McKay	SE 2.25.1	to Sexton 1906
31	Donald Morrison	NW 27.25.2	to Sexton 1906
32	John McKay	NE 2.25.2	to Sexton 1906
74	Malcolm McKay	SE 2.25.2	to Sexton 1906
35	Peter Morrison	NW 34.25.2	to Sexton 1906
36	Donald McDonald	SW 15.25.2	to Sexton 1906
77	Alexander McDonald	SE 15.25.2	to Sexton 1906
77b	John McDonald	NE 10.25.2	to Sexton 1906
96	Mary McDonald	NW 10.25.2	to Sexton 1906

The Lothian Colony (continued)			
Admin. No.	Name of Settler	Location (W2)	Disposition of Land
37	Roderick McKay	NE 9.25.2	to Sexton 1906
78	Angus McKay	NW 14.25.2	to Sexton 1906
39	Ewan MacKay	SW 14.25.2	to son 1905
40	Neil McSween	NW 15.25.2	to Sexton 1906
80	Torlach McSween	NW 22.25.2	to Sexton 1906
42	Alexander Young	NW 1.25.1	to Sexton 1906
82	Norman Morrison	SE 1.25.1	to Sexton 1906
43	Archibald Ferguson	SE 14.25.2	to settler 1908
47	John McIver	SE 13.25.2	to Sexton 1906
85	John McIver (son of #47)	NW 13.25.2	to Sexton 1906
88	Donald McIver	SW 13.25.2	to settler 1905
48	Kenneth McLeod	NW 36.24.1	to Sexton 1906
49	Donald McLeod	SW 18.25.1	to Sexton 1906

Appendix II-b			
ICB Lands Near Saltcoats: The King Colony			
Admin. No.	Name of Settler	Location (W2)	Disposition of Land
1	John McAuley	NE 9.24.3	to non-crofter 1903
3	Donald Montgomery	NW 16.24.3	to non-crofter 1902
52	Duncan Martin	NE 16.24.3	to non-crofter 1902
4	Alexander McDonald	SE 16.24.3	to non-crofter 1902
8	Norman McRae	SW 16.24.3	to non-crofter 1902
9	John McAuley Jr.	NW 9.24.3	to non-crofter 1903
29	Alexander Murray	SE 4.24.3	to non-crofter 1903
30	Alexander Morrison	SE 17.24.3	to non-crofter 1902
33	John McKay Jr.	SE 21.24.3	to non-crofter 1903
75	Donald Murray	SW 22.24.3	to non-crofter 1903
34	John McKay	SW 21.24.3	to non-crofter 1903
38	Murdo McSween	SE 20.24.3	to non-crofter 1902
41	Murdo McDonald	SW 9.24.3	to non-crofter 1903
44	Murdo McIver	NE 17.24.3	to non-crofter 1902
45	Neil McIver	NW 20.24.3	to non-crofter 1902
46	John McDonald	SE 9.24.3	to non-crofter 1903

Sources: SRO, AF 51 files; NA, RG 15, vol. 590, file 198738(1); NA, RG 15, vol. 603, file 21189(1-2); Saskatchewan Homestead Records.

A Note on Sources

Those interested in further particulars of the emigration scheme and of the settlements can consult a wide range of primary sources. The main archival source is the Scottish Record Office's AF 51 series. These files are now available through the National Archives of Canada. The most important Canadian records are those found in RG 15 (Department of the Interior) and RG 76 (Records of the Immigration Branch). A wealth of British government publications are relevant, especially the *Reports of the Imperial Colonisation Board* published in the British Parliamentary Papers 1890-1906.

Two theses pertaining to the scheme are Marilyn Lewry, "A Study of Locational Changes Among Hebridean Immigrants in Southeast Saskatchewan, 1883 to 1926" (University of Regina, 1985) and W. Norton, "The Imperial Colonisation Board, 1888-1909" (University of British Columbia, 1988). John L. Tyman discusses the Pelican Lake settlements in *By Section, Township and Range: Studies in Prairie Settlement* (Brandon: Assiniboine Historical Society, 1972). Related articles include Stuart Macdonald, "Crofter Colonisation in Canada 1886-1892: The Scottish Political Background," *Northern Scotland* 7, no. 1 (1986); Kent Stuart, "The Scottish Crofter Colony, Saltcoats, 1889-1904," *Saskatchewan History* 24, no. 2 (1971); Marilyn Lewry, "The Invisible Partner: The Influence of the Financial Sponsor on the Development of Three Nineteenth Century Hebridean Colonies in Western Canada," *Regina Geographical Studies* 5 (1988); W. Norton, "Malcolm McNeill and the Emigrationist Alternative to Highland Land Reform, 1886-1893," *The Scottish Historical Review* 70, no. 189 (April 1991), and Norton, "'Purely an Imperial Tentative Effort': Canada and the Crofter Colonisation Scheme, 1888-1906," *Prairie Forum* 18, no. 1 (Spring 1993).

Readers interested in the conditions of the Highlands and Islands in late nineteenth-century Scotland are referred to T.M. Devine, *The Great Highland Famine*; James Hunter, *The Making of the Crofting Community*; I.M.M. MacPhail, *The Crofters' War*; and T.C. Smout, *A Century of the Scottish People*.

Local histories should be used with caution, but are always informative about individual settlers. See *Then and Now* (1957), *And So Ninette* (1958), *History of the Riverside Municipality* (1967), *Trails and Crossroads* (1967), *Killarney Reflections* (1982), *Saltcoats: Thunder and Sunshine* (1982), and *Hilton Heritage* (1987).

Notes

Chapter 1: Origins

1. Scottish Record Office (SRO), Lothian Papers, GD 40/16/32, *Confidential Reports to the Secretary for Scotland on the Condition of the Western Highlands and Islands,* 19-20. The reports were submitted to A.J. Balfour in October 1886 by Malcolm McNeill. See p. 7 of this publication.

2. Much has been written on conditions in the Highlands. Recommended are J.M. Bumsted, *The People's Clearance: Highland Emigration to British North America, 1770-1815* (Winnipeg: University of Manitoba Press, 1982); T.M. Devine, *The Great Highland Famine: Hunger, Emigration and the Scottish Highlands in the Nineteenth Century* (Edinburgh: John Donald, 1988); and James Hunter, *The Making of the Crofting Community* (Edinburgh: John Donald, 1976). Scotland's finest social historian places the Highland situation in a broader context: see T.C. Smout, *A Century of the Scottish People, 1830-1950* (New Haven: Yale University Press, 1986).

3. For details of the disturbances, see James Hunter, *The Making of the Crofting Community* and I.M.M. MacPhail, *The Crofters' War* (Stornoway: Acair, 1989).

4. This famous report is found in the British Parliamentary Papers. *Report of Her Majesty's Commissioners of Inquiry into the Condition of the Crofters and Cottars in the Highlands and Islands of Scotland* (the Napier Commission) [C-3980] 1884.

5. Great Britain. *Report of Her Majesty's Commissioners of Inquiry Into the Condition of the Crofters and Cottars in the Highlands and Islands of Scotland* (The Napier Commission) [C-3980] 1884: 3.

6. Great Britain. *Report to the Board of Supervision by John McNeill on the Western Highlands and Islands.* British Parliamentary Papers 1851, xxvi: 908.

7. Malcolm McNeill, "The Crofters: Their Conditions and Prospects," *Blackwood's Edinburgh Magazine* 139 (1889): 527. The term Long Island is commoly used to refer to the Hebrides from Lewis to Barra.

8. Duke of Argyll, "A Corrected Picture of the Highlands," *Nineteenth Century* 16 (1884): 692.

9. National Archives of Canada (NA), RG 25, Records of the Department of External Affairs, vol. 10, John Lowe to D. Beaton, 11 September 1884.

10. In a series of disputes with authorities culminating in January 1883, crofters on the Isle of Skye at Glendale had forcibly expelled police from the region. Those suspected of being the ringleaders, while evading arrest, were known as the Glendale fugitives.

11. Thomas Ferguson, *Scottish Social Welfare* (Edinburgh: E. and S. Livingstone, 1958), 50-52.

12. SRO, GD 40/16/32, Lothian Papers, confidential reports by Malcolm McNeill 1886.

13. SRO, AF 51/6, Charles Tupper to Scottish Office, 17 December 1886.

14. SRO, AF 51/8, Sir George Stephen to Secretary for Scotland, 15 February 1887.

15. SRO, GD 40/16/12/56 and 58.

16. Great Britain. *Report to Her Majesty's Secretary for Scotland on the Condition of the Crofter Population in the Lews* [C 5265] 1888.

17. SRO, AF 51/22.

18. SRO, AF 51/25, Knutsford to Lansdowne, 11 April 1888.

Chapter 2: Departures

1. SRO, AF 51/57, McNeill to Scottish Office, 4 June 1888.

2. SRO, AF 51/34, McNeill to Scottish Office, 4 May 1888.

3. SRO, AF 51/41.

4. The crofters were not the only special group aboard this sailing of the *Corean*. William Quarrier, founder of the Orphan Homes of Scotland, and his wife accompanied a party of over 100 disadvantaged children bound for new homes in Canada.

5. SRO, AF 51/30, Minutes and Correspondence between Scottish Office, Commercial Colonisation Company, and Treasury.

6. SRO, AF 51/35, Scottish Office to Peacock Edwards, 11 May 1888. The involvement of private land companies in placing homesteaders on government lands was common practice. The companies believed that such settlement enhanced the value of their own adjacent lands which were held for sale.

7. SRO, AF 51/56.

8. SRO, AF 51/57.

9. Great Britain. *Report From the Select Committee on Colonisation* [C-274] 1889, 23.

10. SRO, AF 51/93, McNeill to Scottish Office, 8 October 1888.

11. SRO, AF 51/75, P. McLeod to Scottish Office, 10 September 1888.

12. SRO, AF 51/72, Tupper to Scottish Office, 25 October 1888.

13. SRO, AF 51/142, Scottish Office Minute, 16 March 1889.

14. NA, RG 15, Records of the Department of the Interior, vol. 575, file 176811(1), Sir John Thompson to Edgar Dewdney, 29 November 1888.

15. SRO AF 51/188, Colmer to Lothian, 10 April, 1888.

Chapter 3: Arrivals

1. *Manitoba Free Press*, 22 May 1888, 1

2. SRO, AF 51/69, W.B. Scarth to Peacock Edwards, 26 July 1888.

3. SRO, AF 51/58, Edwards to Scottish Office, 19 June 1888.

4. SRO, AF 51/58, Scarth to Edwards, 22 and 26 July 1888.

5. SRO, AF 51/69, "Specimen Details of Advance" for William MacLeod.

6. Glenbow-Alberta Institute Archives, Canada North-West Land Company Papers, vol. 13.

7. Curiously, John Nicolson's brother Kenneth entered for his homestead at SE 25.4.17 using the name John McLean as an alias. It was also discovered that Norman McLennan had not after all emigrated with the Angus MacLeod party. His place had been taken by Alexander Morrison who revealed his identity when he entered for his homestead at NW 27.6.16. The Scottish Office was informed of the anomolies by H.H. Smith's report in November 1888.

8. SRO, AF 51/69, Scarth to Edwards, 26 July 1888.

9. See chapter 4.

10. SRO, AF 51/108, Dewdney to Tupper, 26 November 1888.

11. NA, MG 26 A, John A. Macdonald Papers, vol. 31, W.H. Smith to John A. Macdonald, 22 December 1888.

12. NA, RG 15, vol 575, file 176811(2), report of Grant MacKay, 12 April 1889.

13. SRO, AF 51/198/514, T.J. Lawlor to Sir George Trevelyan, 21 January 1895.

14. NA, RG 15, vol. 590, file 198738(1), Smith to Burgess and Borradaile to Dewdney, 14 April 1889.

15. *Manitoba Free Press*, 25 April 1889, 2

16. C.J. Houston and C. Stuart Houston, eds., *Pioneer of Vision: The Reminiscences of T.A. Patrick, M.D.* (Saskatoon: Western Producer Prairie Books, 1980) 10.

17. Thomas MacNutt was to become MP for Assiniboia East. He was returned as a Liberal in 1908 and 1911, and as a Liberal Unionist in 1917.

18. NA, RG 15, vol. 590, file 198738(1), A.F. Eden to H.H. Smith, 3 July 1889.

19. Marilyn Lewry, *A Study of the Locational Changes Among Hebridean Immigrants in Southeast Saskatchewan* (University of Regina, 1985) 74.

20. NA, RG 15, vol. 590, file 198738(1), Colmer to MacKay, 16 March 1889.

21. *Manitoba Free Press*, 2 July 1889, 2.

22. NA, RG 15, vol 590, file 198738(1), Burgess to Dewdney, 8 July 1889.

23. Ibid., Dewdney to Tupper, 9 July 1889.

24. SRO, AF 51/188/4200/43, Treasury to Scottish Office, 15 August 1889.

25. Great Britain. *Report of the Imperial Colonisation Board* [C6067] 1890, 7. This report was the first of fifteen issued by the ICB. It includes a lengthy appendix by Colmer and details of the circumstances of each family at the time of Colmer's visit.

Chapter 4: Settlements and Administration to 1893

1. SRO, AF 51/98.

2. *The Canadian Gazette* (London), 10 January 1889, 345.

3. SRO, AF 51/199/584.

4. Michael Davitt, "Impressions of the Canadian Northwest," *Nineteenth Century* 31 (1892): 639.

5. *The Visit of the Tenant-Farmer Delegates to Canada in 1890, Part IV* (London: McCorquodale, 1891) 19.

6. NA, Aberdeen Papers, Journals of Lady Aberdeen, Reel C-1352, 7 October 1890.

7. Ibid.

8. Lady Aberdeen, *Through Canada With a Kodak* (Edinburgh: W.H. White, 1893), 110.

9. *Manitoba Free Press*, 8 October 1889, 4.

10. SRO, AF 51/190/4200/108, Colmer to H.H. Smith, 23 July 1890.

11. Great Britain. *Report of the Imperial Colonisation Board* [C-6067] 1890, report of J.G. Colmer, 8.

12. Great Britain. *Report From the Select Committee on Colonisation* [C-354] 1890, 369.

13. Great Britain. *Second Report of the Imperial Colonisation Board* [C-6287] 1890-91 11.

14. NA, RG 13, Records of the Department of Justice, vol. 79, file 1326, Colmer to Dewdney, 1 November 1890.

15. SRO, AF 51/196/438, *Correspondence Respecting the Crofter Settlements*, Robert McKay *et al.* to Trevelyan, 31 May 1893.

16. Ibid., Tupper to Trevelyan, 13 December 1893.

17. Ibid., Borradaile to Colmer, 11 December 1893

18. Ibid., Tupper to Trevelyan, 24 January 1894.

19. Great Britain. *Report From the Select Committee on Colonisation* [C-152] 1891.

20. SRO, AF 51/193/286, Borradaile to Winnipeg-based Subcommittee of the Imperial Colonisation Board, 18 August 1892.

21. Great Britain. *Fourth Report of the Imperial Colonisation Board* [C-7226] 1893, 5.

22. *Manitoba Free Press*, 20 September 1893, 3.

Chapter 5: Settlements and Administration to 1906

1. Andrew Graham paid his debt to the ICB in full in the summer of 1893. He immediately sold his land and returned to Lewis where he died the following year.

2. SRO, AF 51/198/514, T.J. Lawlor to Trevelyan, 21 January 1895.

3. Roderick Mackay had left Harris with £45 in declared private assets in 1888. In 1894, his house was valued by Borradaile at $300, whereas most others were valued at only $10. Within a year of the initiation of legal proceedings, Mackay had paid the ICB $300 on account.

4. Manitoba. *Sessional Papers* 1897, Public Accounts (Sessional Paper No. 12), 117.

5. SRO, AF 51/200/602, Scottish Office Minute, 12 May 1896.

6. SRO, AF 51/202/713, Report by Professor Rankine, 2.

7. NA, RG 15, Records of the Department of the Interior, vol. 590, file 198738(2), Lawlor to Smart, 27 August 1897.

8. *The Killarney Guide*, 12 February 1897, 8.

9. SRO, AF 51/204/834, Scottish Office to Treasury, 8 May 1900.

10. NA, RG 76, Records of the Immigration Branch, vol. 108, file 20013, Speers to Pedley, 16 July 1902.

11. Great Britain. *Fifteenth Report of the Imperial Colonisation Board* [Cd 3145] 1906, 3-4.

12. SRO, AF 51/209/1083, Stewart Tupper to Colmer, 26 February 1909.

13. This unpublished report can be found in SRO, file AF 51/208/1008.

Chapter 6: The Historical Consequences of "Emigration Roulette"

1. Great Britain. *Report From the Select Committee on Colonisation* [C-152] 1890-91.

2. See chapter 3.

3. Canada. *Journals of the House of Commons* (1890), Appendix No. 5, 41.

4. Canada. *Journals of the House of Commons* (1892), Appendix No. 2, 147.

5. City Archives of Vancouver, Alexander Begg's Crofter Immigration Papers, 545-570.

6. Like the crofter immigrants, the settlers brought to the West by the Reverend Isaac Barr in April 1903 were both celebrated and scrutinized by the press. See Lynne Bowen, *Muddling Through: The Remarkable Story of the Barr Colonists* (Vancouver: Douglas and McIntyre, 1992).

7. For the policies followed by Sutherland, Matheson and other Highland landlords, see J.M. Bumsted, *The People's Clearance*; T.M. Devine, *The Great Highland Famine*; and James Hunter, *The Making of the Crofting Community*.

8. The view that the Highland tenant populations were betrayed and victimized has often been compellingly presented. It is appropriate, however, that neither the most famous nor the most recent proponent of this argument has attempted to apply it to the crofter emigrants of 1888 and 1889. See John Prebble, *The Highland Clearances* (London: Secker and Warburg, 1963) and David Craig, *On the Crofters' Trail: In Search of the Clearance Highlanders* (London: Jonathan Cape, 1990).

9. Scarth's calculation derived from his experience with the Canada North-West Land Company and was also the conventional wisdom of the late nineteenth century. Exclusive of Scottish advances and transportation costs, the sums expended on behalf of the family heads fall well short of the minimum capital requirements estimated by Robert Ankli and Robert Litt, and between the estimates of minimum capital requirements and average homestead costs calculated by Lyle Dick. See Robert E. Ankli and Robert M. Litt, "The Growth of Prairie Agriculture: Economic Considerations," in

Donald H. Akenson, ed., *Canadian Papers in Rural History* 1 (1978): 55; and
Lyle Dick, "Estimates of Farm-Making Costs in Saskatchewan, 1882-1914,"
Prairie Forum 6 (1981): 197.

Appendices

1. At Pelican Lake, the administration numbers 1-33 were those assigned by
    Malcolm McNeill to the family heads before they left Scotland. Numbers 3,
    12 and 20 are missing because those families failed to embark. Other
    numbers represent relatives who entered for homesteads and assumed
    responsibility for the family head's debt in excess of $600, as did Samuel
    Graham (no. 54) for his brother-in-law, Donald MacDonald (no. 2), for
    example.

    At Saltcoats, the administration numbers 1-49 were those assigned to the
    family heads upon arrival. Subsequent numbers were given to other family
    members as they entered for homesteads under ICB auspices over the years.

2. The spelling of family names is highly inconsistent in the documents created
    in connection with the settlement scheme. Most of the settlers could sign
    their names only with an "X," leaving successive officials free to adopt a
    variety of spellings. McKinnon, Mackinnon and MacKinnon, for example,
    were applied at various times to both family heads bearing that surname in
    the Argyle colony. Generally speaking, for the purposes of this book, those
    spellings used by Malcolm McNeill on the emigration documents for the
    Pelican Lake settlers have been retained. In the case of the Saltcoats settlers,
    whose emigration documents cannot be located, the spellings used by the
    Department of the Interior officials have been generally followed.

Index